S. F. BARNES

His Life and Times

S. F. BARNES (STAFFORDSHIRE).

Andrew Searle

With a foreword by Rev. Malcolm G. Lorimer

S. F. Barnes
His Life and Times

ANDREW SEARLE

Manchester
EMPIRE PUBLICATIONS

First published in 1997

EMPIRE PUBLICATIONS LTD
62 Charles Street, Manchester M1 7DF

ISBN   1 901746 00 3

 Set in 11 on 13 point Book Antiqua by
Michael Hubbard
and printed in Great Britain
by Manchester Free Press
Longford Trading Estate
Thomas Street
Stretford
Manchester M32 0JT

Art, resolution, stamina, he commanded them all. Well might a man who saw him in his prime have found himself saying: 'Here was Caesar! When comes such another?'

H. S. Altham

Contents

List of Illustrations

Preface

Hanging in the clubhouse at Rishton Cricket Club in Lancashire is a photograph of that club's very first championship-winning team. In 1898 Rishton won the Lancashire League title for the very first time and one man dominated that season and dominates that photograph.

Sydney Francis Barnes had had a fairly undistinguished cricket career up to that point. Already in his mid-20's, he had failed to make the grade with Warwickshire and had turned to league cricket to earn his living. Over the next fifteen years, an era which bestrode the Golden Age of cricket, Barnes became the world's leading bowler and one of its most incredible characters.

I have spent two years researching the life of this remarkable man and have been helped by many people too numerous to mention. My special thanks go to John Ireland and Malcolm Lorimer, whose enthusiasm for the project kept me going. Many thanks to Tony Sheldon for allowing me to use his monumental collection of cricket memorabilia. I would also like to thank the staff at Manchester Central Library for their helpfulness and Mike Hubbard for his patience in turning my words and statistics into book form. Thank you, too, to all those people who must have been driven mad by my obsession with this one man. In the end I feel it was all worthwhile.

Andrew Searle
Manchester

FOREWORD

by Rev. Malcolm G. Lorimer
Hon. Librarian Lancashire C.C.C.

Sydney Barnes was considered by his contemporaries and those who saw him play to be the best bowler the world has seen. This is a quite extraordinary claim and one which Andy Searle backs up in this marvellous book, which aims to shed light on one of cricket's most mysterious and, it could be said, awkward characters. Any description of Barnes gives a hint of what a fearsome bowler he must have been: *"A tall lean man with a predatory look and a cool, calculating brain, an eternal schemer plotting the downfall of batsmen with unrelenting hostility."*

This book seeks to go behind the popular conceptions of Barnes and gets down to questioning just how good a bowler he was. Andy Searle unearths a lot of new material and goes into a great amount of detail relating to his cricket as well as Barnes the man. S.F. Barnes will always remain an enigma: that such a great bowler should play so little County Cricket, choosing to play instead for his own county of Staffordshire and in the leagues where he strode like a colossus.

In an age of Gentlemen and Amateurs, Barnes could be regarded as the true professional; hiring out his services and selling his craft as one would sell the skills of a master mason. I like the story about the charity match in the 1930's when Barnes was in his fifties. Learie Constantine, a great entertainer was being made to struggle for his runs and Cec Parkin, Barnes' captain in the game, realising that a bit of hitting was required to entertain the crowds, turned to Barnes. *"Chuck 'em up to him, Sid,"* he said. *"Let the crowd see him crack one or two."* Barnes threw the ball down, collected his sweater and refused to finish the over or bowl again in the match. As he put on his sweater he turned to Parkin and said tersely: *"I have a reputation as well as Constantine."* The master refusing to compromise his craft!

After reading this book the name of S.F. Barnes looms even larger, one of the most enigmatic of cricketers and one whose mystery and exploits still live on.

1.

THE MAKING OF A LEGEND

It is November 1901. The Orient steamer 'Omrah' sails through a storm-lashed Bay of Biscay on a six-week odyssey from England to Australia. This journey was one of the great sea journeys, repeated many times since Captain Arthur Philip set sail with eleven ships and a cargo of convicted felons in 1787. But despite the experience of over a century of sea-faring between these two distant outposts of the British Empire, it was still a journey fraught with danger from the elements.

Amongst the passengers on this adventure to the other side of the world was a very special group of men. A party of fourteen of England's finest cricketers were to spend the next four months attempting to win back that most glorious of all cricket trophies: The Ashes. It was not by any means a team of experienced travellers. Even though this was the fifteenth such tour to leave for the Australasian continent since such visits began in 1862 - and the fourth in ten years - only two of the party had previously made such a trip. Of this pair, Archibald Campbell MacLaren, Captain of Lancashire and England, was making his third sojourn to a country for which he had a particular affection: He had enjoyed great success there as a batsman on his two previous tours and had met and married his wife, Maud, during his first visit.

It was to MacLaren that this talented but youthful team turned when the weather worsened. A storm had been raging for what seemed like weeks but was, in fact, just days. The ship's captain's announcement that worse was to follow struck a fear into MacLaren's charges a hundred times greater than the thought of facing Australia's finest in the forthcoming Test series. It was a naive group of men, many of whom had experienced little of the world; a world which had reached a new millennium and had recently seen the death Queen Victoria, that great figurehead of the British Empire's hegemony of the previous Century.

Archie MacLaren had seen it all before and was looking forward to meeting and matching old foes. Fearless and successful in the previous decade and one of the truly great heroes of what was developing into cricket's 'Golden Age', MacLaren, attempting to comfort one of his petrified young charges, exclaimed wryly:

If we do go down, at least that bugger Barnes
will go down with us!

Why did the eminent Maclaren make such a comment about one of his players? What sort of man was this *"bugger Barnes"*? Was this comment merely a jokey aside, or an insight into a wider truth that a collection of fourteen sportsmen and egos had already deduced after just a few days in rough seas? The truth is all this and more because, without a shadow of a doubt, Sydney Francis Barnes was the greatest of all the enigmas to emerge from cricket's Golden Age.

When one looks at the period between 1890 and 1914 one sees a world gearing up for the greatest conflict in its history. Technological advances had brought the development of weapons of mass destruction; new alliances were formed between nation states which made war inevitable; international crises became the norm. Governments postured; peoples prepared for the glorious slaughter.

Cricket, meanwhile, enjoyed its greatest era. The game grew, not only in popularity, but also in technical and innovatory excellence. Of all cricket's ages those twenty or so years before the Great War produced a succession of geniuses unparalleled in any other walk of life or popular pastime in any other era. In the County Championship there was, at Gloucestershire, that most recognisable of all Victorians, W.G.Grace. Although in the twilight of his career he was still a formidable cricketer and personality. His county colleague, Gilbert Jessop, was the most attacking batsman of his generation. At Lancashire there was Archie MacLaren, according to Neville Cardus *"the noblest Roman of them all"*, supported by that most accomplished of all professionals J.T.Tyldesley. 'The Prince' Ranjitsinhji and that magnificent all-round sportsman C.B.Fry graced the cricket fields of Sussex. George Hirst and Wilfred Rhodes, all-rounders par excellence, kept Yorkshire at the top of the tree. At the Oval, Surrey possessed Tom Richardson and Bill Lockwood, the country's leading seam bowlers, whilst the great Jack Hobbs

3

was soon to make his appearance. Australia, not to be outdone, was a production line of genius: Joe Darling, Monty Noble, Clem Hill, Syd Gregory, Hugh Trumble, Reggie Duff, Charlie Macartney, Warwick Armstrong and the majestic Victor Trumper.

These were but a few of the glorious cricketers and characters that made this period truly cricket's Golden Age. That Sydney Barnes emerged suddenly and without warning on an unsuspecting cricket world at this time is indisputable. For the making of the legend one must travel just a few months back in time from that torrid sea journey to Australia and to the final throes of the 1901 County Championship.

The Summer of 1901 produced some marvellous cricket. It was the best Summer for batsmanship since the County Championship's official inauguration in 1890; a Summer unparalleled until well after the First World War. No less than four players topped 2,000 runs. At the head of the first class averages were the two imperious Sussex amateurs, Ranjitsinhji and Fry. The professionals of Lancashire and Surrey respectively, Tyldesley and Hayward, were the other pair to pass the 2,000-run landmark; a landmark which had been reached just four times in total in the first twelve seasons of the County Championship. In fact, the bat had so outflanked the ball in 1901 that no less than ten players averaged over fifty.

Victory in the County Championship, however, had gone to Yorkshire. They had won twenty of their twenty-seven championship fixtures thanks to two bowlers who were head and shoulders above any others in the country. Wilfred Rhodes, with 196 wickets, and George Hirst, with 135, had devoured even the strongest of batting teams at home and away all season long. Middlesex finished as runners- up, whilst Archie MacLaren's Lancashire were a close third. For the previous six seasons Yorkshire had dominated the championship, winning it on four occasions, with Lancashire, the 1897 champions, their closest rivals. The Roses matches at this time were lively, noisy, well-patronised occasions, with an intense rivalry still prevalent today. The Lancashire batting was very strong, with MacLaren and the excellent Tyldesley to the fore. However, their bowling had fallen away dramatically due to the unfortunate premature retirement of Johnny Briggs, due to a seizure which led to his death in early 1902, and the withdrawal of their stalwart quick bowler of the previous decade, Arthur Mold, halfway through the 1901 season after he had been no-balled for throwing. This desire to beat Yorkshire and win the County Championship led to the acquisition of Sydney Barnes.

The loss of Briggs and Mold, both international cricketers, had been keenly felt at Old Trafford, so when MacLaren heard of the prolific feats of a certain fast/medium bowler called Barnes at Burnley in the Lancashire League he invited him to play in the final County Championship fixture of the season at Old Trafford against Leicestershire. In the first innings, bowling beautifully with a wonderful high action, superb control of length and line, and moving the ball prodigiously off the wicket, he returned the excellent figures of six for 70. Thanks to this display he was awarded a contract for the following season at Old Trafford and, in a move which was to have greater significance for the future dealings of Sydney Barnes with the financial administrators of both Lancashire and the M.C.C., the county club paid Burnley one hundred pounds to release him from his 1902 contract. He was twenty-eight years old.

At twenty-eight Barnes was no overnight sensation. In fact, he had played county cricket before. Born in Smethwick, Staffordshire on the 19th April 1873, he began by playing for his home-town team in the Birmingham League, thus attracting the attentions of Warwickshire, for whom he made a handful of appearances between 1893 and 1896. Having made little impact he joined Rishton in the

Lancashire League as a professional, resulting in Lancashire's interest. He appeared twice for the county in 1899, without creating much of an impression. By 1901, however, Barnes had become a seasoned professional, developing his special talent to such a degree that his phenomenal success in the Lancashire League was guaranteed to bring him to the attention of the Lancashire club, especially with their bowling resources depleted by the end of the careers of Briggs and Mold.

How Barnes ended up on the S.S. Omrah with MacLaren and his England team after a mere half dozen moderately successful county games over seven seasons is the stuff of legend. Much has been made of Archie MacLaren's role in the Barnes story. The apocryphal tale is that Barnes turned up at the nets at Old Trafford to bowl at MacLaren. At the time Archie MacLaren was seen as one of the greatest all-round batsmen in the world. When Barnes bowled he is supposed to have apologised profusely after constantly hitting MacLaren about the gloves and pads. MacLaren - so the story goes - is quoted as describing the encounter thus:

He thumped me on the left thigh. He hit my gloves from a length. He actually said, 'Sorry, Sir!' and I said, 'Don't be sorry Barnes, you're coming to Australia with me.'

As will become apparent later in the Barnes story, this particular anecdote can be ruled out as purely a flight of fancy. Barnes apologised to no one - least of all a batsman - whilst MacLaren himself was too shrewd a judge of a cricketer to take the evidence of net practice as justification to include someone in an England team for an arduous tour of Australia. Wisden is nearer the mark in its 1903 edition when it recalls the choice of Barnes:

He was so successful against Leicestershire, and earned such a high reputation at Burnley, both as a bowler and a batsman, that Mr MacLaren, being hard pressed for bowling talent, invited him to join the team for Australia.

The truth is that when Wisden describes MacLaren as *"hard pressed for bowling talent"*, this was due to one man. This individual, who was most responsible for the selection of Barnes for the 1901/2 tour of Australia, was none other than the captain of the champion county. Lord Hawke, the self-styled guardian of Yorkshire cricket first and English cricket second and last, is the most important element in the Barnes story. It is said of Hawke, quite accurately as will be observed as the Barnes story unfolds, that he lost more Test matches than any other man who has never played for England. The writer and journalist Benny Green, in his superbly prosaic book 'A History of Cricket', appropriately describes him as *"the bear of little brain"*. It is entirely possible that without the intervention of this long-term dictator of Yorkshire cricket Sydney Francis Barnes may never have played a single Test match and the incredible records he was to create over the next twelve years - some of which still stand today - may never have been indelibly etched into the record books.

After the 1901/2 tour the M.C.C. took over the organisation and selection of teams to play abroad, but up until then it was incumbent upon the captain to select a touring squad. In this instance it was the job of MacLaren, as the current England captain, to assemble a team strong enough to return the Ashes back to England for the first time since 1896. Naturally MacLaren wanted the strongest possible team, so Rhodes and Hirst, the two Yorkshire bowlers who had performed so splendidly in 1901, were selected. Lord Hawke, not for the first time nor the last putting parochialism before patriotism, vetoed their selection in the name of

Yorkshire cricket. His facile reasoning was that both Rhodes and Hirst were too tired after an exacting season, and that a long and wearying trip to Australasia would see them completely ruined for the 1902 season and Yorkshire's defence of the County Championship title. At this point it would be appropriate to quote the opinion of the Middlesex and future England batsman and captain Pelham Warner, a man whose views generally, as an amateur of the same ilk as Hawke, would not usually be out of kilter with those of the Yorkshire bombast. Warner comments as follows:

Yorkshire's reasons for refusing permission was that a tour in Australia would wear out Hirst and Rhodes, and Yorkshire cricket would thereby suffer. I have never been able to understand why a tour in Australia should impair in any way the subsequent efficiency and stamina of any cricketer, and especially two such physically fit and strong men. Surely there are no hardships to be undergone when one begins with a five to six weeks' voyage on a luxurious liner and ends with another voyage of the same duration? Again, the lovely Australian climate, if occasionally a little too hot, is surely better for anyone's health than a winter in Briggate or Lascelles Hall?

The irony of Warner's comments is that Lord Hawke almost certainly believed this was true because, just two years later, Hirst and Rhodes both went on the next tour to Australia. But that was under the auspices of the M.C.C. and not under the leadership of a man with whom Hawke was to have one of the most damaging feuds in Test cricket history. For the real reason why Hawke refused to consent to Hirst and Rhodes' inclusion in the party was a clash of egos of titanic proportions between himself and MacLaren, which had first been displayed in 1899, was to fester and ferment in 1902, and reached its ultimate manifestation in 1909 with probably the most destructive piece of selectorial incompetence in Test match cricket history.

Hawke and MacLaren, both "amateurs" and "gentlemen", would never allow national pride and the successful conduct of international cricket to restrict the application of their own selfish interests. As Warner states further: *"Naturally MacLaren resented Yorkshire's attitude, and a good deal of friction resulted, Maclaren thinking that he had been badly treated by Yorkshire, or, rather, by Lord Hawke, who was Yorkshire."* There was no love lost between the pair but MacLaren seems to occupy the moral high ground. He saw Hawke, quite correctly, as an inferior cricketer in a superior Yorkshire team. This is proven by Hawke's career average of twenty, as opposed to MacLaren's thirty-three. And, whereas MacLaren saw it as his duty to put his county's resources at the disposal of his country, Hawke's actions - more often than not - had Yorkshire's rather than the national interests at heart. It is ironic, therefore, that in 1902, despite Yorkshire's retention of the championship, neither Hirst nor Rhodes were as effective as in the previous year.

All this, apart from revealing the grand self-interest at play in the cricket world, merely served to propagate the extraordinary career of Sydney Barnes. His addition as the fourteenth and final member of Archie MacLaren's party for the 1901/2 tour of Australia in the middle of September created hoots of derision from the London-based press. Quite correctly they pointed to Barnes' lack of experience. Just a handful of moderately successful first class games was no recommendation, they argued, for a bowler to tour Australia with the aim of recovering the Ashes, a trophy that the cream of English cricket had relinquished by four games to one in Australia in 1897/8 and failed to recapture in England in 1899.

Furthermore, the rest of the bowling attack, without the skills of Rhodes and Hirst, was woefully inexperienced. Gilbert Jessop had played just one Test, whilst Len Braund and Colin Blythe, like Barnes, were yet to make their debuts. Jessop, Braund and Blythe, however, had proved themselves in the daily grind of the county circuit; Barnes had proved nothing. To the southern-based newspaper industry he was a league cricketer whose successes had been gained in a sub-standard form of the game. The selection of Sydney Barnes was criticised as yet another example of the idiosyncratic captaincy of Archie MacLaren, whom they had not really forgiven for failing to recover the Ashes in 1899. One London paper even suggested that MacLaren should be consigned to a lunatic asylum. For the press the cry was: *"Who is Barnes?"* They were soon to find out.

The real circumstances surrounding Barnes' inclusion in the touring party followed the county game against Leicestershire. *"That man is a fine bowler. I'm going to ask him to join my team to Australia,"* MacLaren is reported to have told some of his senior players after Barnes' six-wicket haul. When the experienced Lancashire batsman Albert Ward asked Barnes: *"Has MacLaren said anything about going to Australia?"* Barnes was flabbergasted, clearly believing it was a typical piece of dressing-room humour. Moreover, after receiving a telegram inviting him to tour during a Lancashire League game a few weeks later Barnes thought it was a continuation of the ruse. It was only when Joe Allan, his Burnley captain, ordered him off the field to accept the offer that Barnes knew it was no joke. Incidentally, this is the last recorded occasion of Sydney Barnes taking orders off anyone.

On the boat out to Australia Barnes asked MacLaren why he had been selected, pointing out that he hadn't even seen a Test match - let alone thought of playing in one - and that he wasn't a fast bowler. MacLaren shrewdly replied: *"You're fast enough for what I want, Barnes."* Evidently this was a new experience for MacLaren, having a player claim that maybe he wasn't good enough, or the right type of player, for the team. *"I think we shall get on well together,"* said

MacLaren. *"I would much rather a man say what he thinks than be a 'yes' man and then go away and grouse with the others."* Barnes then gave MacLaren a taste of what the cricket administrators of England were to experience time and again over the next twenty years: *"I shall never do that. If I don't agree with you I shall say so."*

Although MacLaren has been repeatedly described as pig-headed, and his tactics often seemed dubious, his decision to take Sydney Barnes to Australia was due to sound common sense. With Hirst and Rhodes unavailable he needed a bowler with the ability to exploit the type of wickets and conditions that would be encountered there. Having already toured Australia twice before, with some degree of success as 728 Test match runs at an average of 40.44 testified, MacLaren was as qualified as anybody in county cricket at that time to decide which bowlers would make an impact. With the enforced unavailability of both Hirst and Rhodes, MacLaren had a hunch that Barnes would be ideally suited to Australian conditions after seeing him perform against Leicestershire. It was one of the most inspired hunches of all time.

AN ENGLISH CARTOONIST'S IMPRESSION OF ENTHUSIASTIC BARRACKING AT SYDNEY CRICKET GROUND, FIRST TEST, 1901.

2.

BARNES IN AUSTRALIA

Sydney Barnes took Australia by storm. Over the next three months he appeared in three Test matches and a number of state games. In the Tests he took nineteen wickets at a cost of only seventeen runs apiece. These figures seem more miraculous on closer examination. In the third Test at Adelaide he bowled just seven wicketless overs due to a serious knee injury which curtailed his tour. In the other four innings in which he bowled, he took five wickets or more in an innings on no less than three occasions, creating his first Test record along the way. *"Such a thought a month ago,"* Barnes was later to write about his selection for the tour, *"would have been ridiculous, but here I was about to take part in the greatest of all matches against Australia in Australia."* Apart from revealing a certain amount of modesty not always apparent in his cricket career, this statement surely shows that Sydney Barnes was not about to pass up this opportunity of a lifetime.

There is a famous cartoon that appeared in an English newspaper after the first Test match in Sydney during the 1903/4 tour to Australia. Clem Hill had been given run out by Umpire Crockett in Australia's second innings whilst he and Victor Trumper were successfully attempting to wipe out a large first innings deficit. The crowd began a demonstration when Hill showed his disgust with the decision by his demeanour walking from the wicket to the pavilion. The crowd's response to Hill's evident disagreement

13

with Crockett's decision almost led to the England captain, Pelham Warner, taking his team off the field. The cartoon has the batsman dressed in a suit of armour, the fielders hidden under manholes and the umpire in a cage, whilst the scoreboard keeps track of the numbers killed and injured. A selection of weapons - including bottles and rocks - is seen showering onto the field. The cartoonist describes the scene as, *"Enthusiastic barracking at Sydney Cricket Ground."* Although this cartoon followed a particularly famous incident it was by no means unusual behaviour by certain elements of the crowd at Sydney. It was in this type of atmosphere that this young and inexperienced England team began the first Test at Sydney on December 13th, 1901.

It was a remarkable start to the Test series for England. MacLaren won the toss and batted on a perfect wicket, promptly setting about the bowling with genuine relish. The experienced Australian trio of Jones, Noble and Trumble were treated with disdain by the England batsmen - particularly MacLaren, who hit a wonderful century. Tom Hayward, with 69, and the wicketkeeper Lilley, with 84, were the other top scorers in a huge total of 464, which was considered at the time to make England almost unbeatable. Barnes played a significant part in that innings. Coming in at number ten, and with the score at 405 for eight, he shared in partnerships of twenty and thirty-nine for the ninth and tenth wicket, eventually finishing undefeated on twenty-six. As this was to be Barnes' second highest Test innings one can only conclude that by this stage the Australians' heads had dropped, allowing him an extended stay at the crease in order to experience the unique atmosphere of Test match cricket in Sydney - although there is evidence that he was more of a batsman than his average at the highest level indicates.

A confident and bullish England team took the field for the start of Australia's first innings. Barnes, urged on by his captain, proceeded to rip the heart out of the Australian batting. Bowling unchanged for almost the entire innings, he sent down 35.1 overs, of which nine were maidens, and took five wickets for 65 runs. Ably supported by Colin Blythe, Kent's young left arm spinner, who took three for 26, and the Somerset seamer Len Braund, with two for 40, Australia were shot out for 168, almost 300 runs short of England's total. It was an extraordinary performance from this unheralded and inexperienced England team - and especially by Barnes. To truly examine the impact of Sydney Barnes in this his first Test match one must look at that Australian innings and see the calibre of batsman that capitulated to his bowling.

There is no doubt that Sydney Barnes set the tone, not only for England's victory but also for his own Test career, with his first ever victim in Test cricket. Only three runs had been scored when Barnes deceived Victor Trumper with guile and flight, inducing him to give a simple return catch. It was a catch which Barnes took casually one-handed, to which MacLaren is reported to have chastised his opening bowler with: *"For God's sake, next time you get a catch like that, get both hands to it!"* Barnes replied, contemptuously: *"Well, I caught it, didn't I?"* *"Yes,"* agreed a ruffled MacLaren, *"but you might have missed it and he might have got 200!"*

When it comes to identifying the greatest batsman of all time Trumper's name always appears in the lists of experts alongside those of Bradman, Hutton, Macartney, Hobbs, Sobers and Richards. In the 1902 season that immediately followed this series Trumper strode majestically around the county grounds of England to score over 2,500 runs - and that in an extremely damp season when most batsmen struggled to dominate the ball. Trumper had already introduced himself as one of the world's finest batsmen on his first tour to England in 1899 with a memorable undefeated 135 at Lord's, which enabled Australia to win that Test by ten wickets and, consequently, the series one-nil. In Australia, however, in that balmy period straddling 1901 and 1902, the great Victor Trumper was made to look a mere mortal in the face of the supreme skills of Sydney Francis Barnes. In fact, in twenty Tests against Australia, Barnes was to dismiss the great man on no less than thirteen occasions, a remarkable feat considering Trumper's undoubted status as one of the greatest batsmen of all time.

After the dismissal of Trumper, the Australian innings settled down with Syd Gregory and Clem Hill beginning to come to terms with the England attack, adding eighty-six before Barnes struck again to end this embryonic partnership. This time it was Clem Hill, a man who had averaged over fifty in his two previous series against England and who would average over fifty in the current one, who succumbed to the wiles of Barnes, bowled for forty-six. Hill, also considered one of the greatest batsmen of the Golden Age, was to fall to Barnes on eleven occasions. This was to prove the decisive wicket as Blythe then made inroads into the middle order. Once again a partnership developed; this time with Australia's skipper Joe Darling, already established as one of the world's premier batsmen, looking set for a long innings. Once again it was Barnes who made the breakthrough, inducing Darling to give a simple catch to Quaife for thirty-nine. To finish the innings, and complete the first of his twenty-four five-wicket hauls in Test cricket, Barnes had Ernest Jones caught by Jessop.

Australia followed on 296 runs adrift and fared little better second time around. This time it was Braund (five for 61) and Blythe (four for 30) who did the damage. Australia, hustled out for 172, had lost by an innings and 124 runs. An outstanding and distinguished Australian team had been steamrollered by a bowling attack whose sum total of Test match experience amounted to a single game. Sydney Barnes can be forgiven his second innings performance; his sixteen overs went for seventy-four runs; his only wicket being that of Trumble, whose stubborn resistance he broke late in the game. Barnes had drained himself during his marathon first innings' effort in the hot weather. He was exhausted, but it was his exertions in Australia's first innings which gave England the impetus for this magnificent victory.

He was hailed - not only back in England - but also in Australia. His brand of aggression and skill went down well with Australian audiences. In fact, his performance had come as no surprise to the crowd at Sydney because he had already announced himself with some superb displays in the State games which had led up to the Test match. Against South Australia in Adelaide he had taken four for 32 and one for 34, and at Sydney, just prior to the first Test, two for 83 and three for 105 against the strong New South Wales team. These two performances would have been considered ample evidence of an emerging international-class bowler, but he had completely stunned the Australian public with match figures of twelve for 99 against Victoria at Melbourne in between the other two state games. It was an exhibition which led many Australians to believe they were witnessing the best bowler that had ever appeared in Australia.

If Barnes' Test debut was to be considered outstanding, his performance in the second Test at Melbourne, which began on New Year's Day 1902, was a tour-de-force. Batting first, Australia lost Trumper in Barnes' opening over, caught by Tyldesley for a duck. Clem Hill, once again bowled by Barnes, was the next to go with the score on 34. Then Blythe gave Barnes support from the other end, dismissing Darling, Noble and Gregory in quick succession, to leave the Aussies floundering on 38 for five. A partnership developed between Trumble and Duff before Barnes blew away the tail, taking the last four wickets for less than twenty runs scored. Australia were all out for 112; Barnes had taken six for 42, Blythe had weighed in with four for 64, and the England team were naturally cock-a-hoop.

Their euphoria, however, was to end here. This was the high point of the entire 1901/2 tour because it was at this stage that England's fortunes took a dramatic downward turn. In just 15.4 overs England were bowled out for a mere 61. In unfavourable conditions MacLaren had ordered his batsmen to get some quick runs so that Barnes could have another go at the Australians before the day was out. Only Jessop, with a fiery twenty-seven, and Maclaren, with thirteen, reached double figures. For Australia, Monty Noble produced the startling analysis of seven wickets for 17 runs off 7.4 overs, receiving good support from Trumble with three for 38. It was a humbling experience for a so far triumphant England team, and it showed when they came out to bowl again in Australia's second innings. The Aussies, back to their best, piled up a total of 353 to lead by an invincible 404 runs.

It was Sydney Barnes who strove the hardest to rectify what had happened in that disastrous England innings. His figures speak for themselves. When Wisden, in its review of the tour, described Barnes as *"overworked"* in this innings it is one of the under-statements of all time. For he bowled sixty-four six-ball overs, the most balls bowled by an individual bowler in a Test innings up to that point. Seventeen of those overs were maidens, whilst his figures for the innings were a marvellous seven wickets for 121 runs. It was an unprecedented effort in Melbourne's heat and humidity and he very nearly turned the game back England's way in the course of this mammoth bowling stint. With the wickets of Trumper cheaply (again), Darling cheaply (again), Trumble cheaply (again) and Gregory cheaply (again), he had been instrumental in reducing Australia to 48 for five and England were in with a chance of victory. But this time Barnes did not receive the required support from Blythe and Braund and the Australians had cleverly changed round their batting order with the wicket playing so many tricks on that evening. The following day Hill (99) and Duff (104) combined to grasp the initiative, and it was only Barnes' expertise with the old ball (the same ball was used throughout an innings at this time in Test cricket) which prevented the deficit climbing beyond the 500 mark. England were dismissed for 175 in their second innings and the Test was lost by 229 runs.

The extent of Sydney Barnes' impact on this game cannot be under-estimated. His match figures were thirteen for 163, a performance only bettered in Ashes Tests for England by W.Bates on the same ground in 1882/3. It was unfortunate that his achievement was upstaged by that of Noble, who took six for 60 in England's second innings to finish with match figures of thirteen for 77. Sydney Barnes, in the space of two Test matches, had established himself as one of the greatest bowlers in the world. A long Test career looked certain even though his tour was now to come to an untimely conclusion. His efforts in this game, in the heat and on the hard Melbourne wicket, took its toll. He developed knee trouble and, although MacLaren decided he was a risk worth taking for the third Test in Adelaide a fortnight later, the writing was on the wall. His tour ended when he limped out of the game after bowling just seven ineffective overs. Not for the first time in his career Barnes had bowled himself into the ground for his team. The series was over as a contest. In Adelaide Australia won by four wickets, at Sydney again they triumphed by seven wickets, and in the final Test in Melbourne they won a close contest by thirty-two runs.

The narrowness of these victories suggests that a fit Barnes may well have swung the Ashes England's way, for Blythe and Braund struggled during the rest of the Australian season without his support. In each of the final three Tests England held the advantage on the first innings, so it would be correct to assume that Barnes, considering the way he had bowled at the beginning of each Australian innings in the first two Tests, would have made the necessary breakthroughs and the Ashes may have reverted back to

19

England. There is, however, an alternative opinion which must be taken into account. Sydney Smith, who was later to become a respected Secretary of the Australian Board of Control for International Cricket says, in his excellent anthology of pre-Second World War Ashes series, 'History of The Tests', the England team *"was not really as representative of English cricket as it should have been...as several players of international class declined the invitation. But..."*, Smith goes on to say about Sydney Barnes' phenomenal performances: *"MacLaren's opinion of this player was fully justified, as he afterwards became one of the greatest bowlers England has produced,"* before adding, *"but he was temperamental."*

Smith, therefore, an Australian who can have no axe to grind, especially after seeing Barnes' majestic bowling in the first two Tests, hints at the essential truth about Sydney Francis Barnes. When one adds it to MacLaren's joking comment on the journey out to Australia about Barnes being a victim should the boat sink, one can begin to visualise the Barnes character. He was a difficult man to play with. A great bowler, certainly, but a man who was as likely to upset his own team as much as the opposition. Patrick Morrah describes him as *"not remarkable for joie de vivre. He was dour, intense, unsmiling, quick to take offence"*, whilst the distinguished cricket historian H.S.Altham explains that Barnes varied *"between days of irresistible success and others, when his temperament got the better of him, with disastrous results."*

One can just visualise the scene now. Australia 48 for five in the second innings of that Melbourne Test and Barnes - carrying an injury - is striving manfully to bowl out the opposition in the heat and humidity, with little or no support from his fellow bowlers. Even at almost a hundred years distance one can see an exasperated Barnes berating his colleagues for their profligacy with the ball and in the field during the partnership between Hill and Duff. Half a century later John Hartley of The Times wrote: *"It is many years since Australian mothers frightened naughty children with the name of Sydney Barnes"*, evoking an image of a man of almost ogre-like ferocity.

Furthermore, a school of thought developed that his breakdown in the third Test, an event which was to find an uncanny resonance at many times during his career, was not quite as serious as Barnes made out. He was naturally disappointed that his efforts had gone unrewarded with victory at Melbourne and, as we shall see time and again in his cricket career, his mood was influenced by the relative success of the team in which he was playing. Wisden makes this cryptic comment:

It has been said that if he had gone on playing his knee would have proved equal to the strain, and confirmation of this view can be found in his experiences after he returned to England, but on this point we cannot, in the absence of any exact knowledge, express an opinion.

Bernard Hollowood, a former Editor of the satirical magazine 'Punch' and a minor counties cricketer of some repute for Staffordshire, played alongside Sydney Barnes in the twilight of his career. He adds further credence to the image of Barnes as a malingerer: *"Put on to bowl at the 'wrong' end, he would scowl and sulk and develop mysterious physical disorders, sprains and strains."* Certainly, he seems to have had a remarkably long career, playing at a high standard well into his sixties, and having his most effective period in Test matches in his early forties, for someone prone to so many injuries. Hollowood provides one of the most entertaining - and enlightening - descriptions of Sydney Barnes the cricketer some thirty years after his historic first appearances in Test cricket. It goes a long way to understanding how Barnes, despite his longevity, successfully managed to convince captains at international, county, minor county and league levels that he was unfit to bowl:

One corner of the changing-room was roped off by his paraphernalia, his shirts, liniments, embrocations, bandages, elastic supports; and a fearful odour seeped from this clutter. It was the smell of hospitals. I looked for formaldehyde and other embalming fluids, for crutches, wooden legs and scars of operations.

It can be argued, therefore, that this England team, lacking experience not only of Australian conditions but also of Test match cricket, performed heroics to run this great Australian side close in those final three Tests. In addition, it can be said that Barnes' presence could have led to bigger defeats, as evidenced by the second Test, despite his undoubted bowling skills. Sydney Smith further explains that after breaking down in that third Test, *"for the remainder of the tour he was of little use to the side,"* suggesting an inactive Barnes had a detrimental effect on morale. It is an indictment which follows Barnes around throughout his cricket career, the more convincing by its constant repetition.

Interestingly, though, Barnes went to see a Harley Street specialist, Dr Wharton Hood, on his return to England after breaking down at the beginning of Lancashire's first match at Lord's against the M.C.C. Hood, who had known of Barnes' problem, as shown by his comment: *"I knew you'd be coming to me eventually, I've been following your case,"* recommended that Barnes have a cartilage removed. Barnes was sure that this was not the problem and ended up going to Glasgow to see an old collier called Blantyre Ray, who was recommended to him by several sportsmen whom he had treated. He found that Barnes had twisted the sinews in the back of his knee and merely untwisted them. *"If I'd been on the ground when it happened, you could have been playing again in ten minutes,"* said the the Glaswegian miracle man and Barnes was able to bowl after a fashion throughout the 1902 season.

Barnes, nevertheless, had made his mark in international cricket. On the balance of probability his bowling could well have swung the series England's way. Over the next decade he was to become the best bowler that had ever played in Australia, taking a further fifty-eight Test wickets on two other tours. The party returned to England in April, accompanied by the Australian touring team, for what promised and proved to be a titanic struggle in the English summer of 1902. After just three Test matches Sydney Barnes had already established himself as a world-class bowler.

3.

THE SUMMER OF 1902

The Summer of 1902 was hardly a summer at all, for it goes down in the record books as one of the wettest in living memory. Only Trumper, of all those great practitioners in the art of batsmanship at the peak of their powers by 1902, prospered on that season's wet and sticky wickets. Trumper mastered all wickets and all conditions to score 2,570 runs, including twelve centuries, at an average of forty-nine. Apart from the majestic Australian there was to be no repeat of the glorious run-feast of the previous season.

Barnes and MacLaren had returned from Australia with their reputations greatly enhanced despite the heavy defeats in the Tests. The former was hailed as the best English bowler seen in Australia up to that point, easily heading the Test averages, and taking forty-one wickets in total in the first class games of his truncated tour, whilst the latter had topped the batting averages with 412 runs at 45.77. MacLaren had been fully vindicated in his selection of Barnes and, at the same time, had led a weakened team with a certain amount of savoir-faire, always pushing for victory even when the odds were stacked against him.

Though 1902 was the wettest summer for a long time, the Test series proved to be one of the most riveting ever. Australia were victorious by two games to one, winning easily at Sheffield, whilst the last two Tests at Old Trafford and the Oval were shared one apiece in two of the most

24

enthralling encounters that have ever taken place between the two countries. England had the better of a rain-affected game at Edgbaston, but the game at Lord's was almost a complete washout. Before we examine the Test series, and Barnes' part in it, let us first take a look at the prelude to the County Championship of 1902 and Barnes' first full season as a contracted county cricketer.

John Kay, in his book on the history of Lancashire County Cricket Club, writes: *"It is fair to assume that if MacLaren had not been captain at the time, Barnes would never have bothered to play for his county or for his country - a tragic waste of the best possible cricketing talent."* Although this may be a fair assessment of his selection for England, the same cannot be said of his appearance in the Lancashire XI of 1902. This is because MacLaren came close to not playing at all for Lancashire in 1902, going instead to Hampshire, whereas Barnes had already signed a contract and would almost certainly have honoured it despite the absence of his mentor. The two men had an obvious mutual respect for each other's expertise but - as already evidenced - MacLaren's respect for Barnes did not extend to the character of the man.

Archie MacLaren was a man to whom officialdom were a body to be endured rather than enjoyed; a trait soon to be displayed in Sydney Barnes. He had been upset with the Lancashire hierarchy's handling of certain affairs during the 1901 season, particularly the parlous state of the Old Trafford wicket, and had been disappointed with the team's erratic performances. Before he left for Australia he resigned the captaincy in a huff, a decision which was accepted with startling alacrity by the Lancashire Committee. Furthermore, MacLaren's wife had become ill and wanted to go down south to be near her sister in Woking and away from Manchester's notoriously damp weather. In a letter to the Club Secretary, Sam Swire, he resigned and announced his intention to play for Hampshire. After the tour to Australia, however, MacLaren's mood - and his wife's health - had been revived to such an extent that he announced his intention to remain at Old Trafford - much to the relief of Sydney Barnes one can safely say in hindsight.

Barnes, though, had problems of his own at the start of the 1902 season. The question of his qualification for the county looked like it was to become a delicate issue. The rules at the time were peculiar to say the least and open to abuse, both by counties hoping to include an experienced mercenary and by the authorities hoping to punish a truculent cricketer or a confrontational county committee. In the early 1880's Lancashire had lost two accomplished bowlers, John Crossland and George Nash, on the pretence of being disqualified from playing for the county, when, in fact, the real reason was the suspect nature of their bowling actions following complaints from other counties. Barnes was summoned before the Committee after the county had received a letter from the M.C.C. telling them not to play him *"because we know he is not qualified for Lancashire"*. His reply - typical of the man - was to say that he was as qualified as some he could mention. And, indeed, his experience of playing for Warwickshire even though born in Staffordshire seems to have bore this out. He was right of course, even if the Lancashire Committee, made up primarily of the type of "gentlemen" who governed the game at this time, were too fearful of his ire to tell him he was wrong. Residential qualification was abused at most county clubs and Barnes, having played in the Lancashire League and lived in the county for a number of years, was as qualified as anyone else. Lancashire, as was often the case during this period, chose to ignore the authorities at Lord's.

If MacLaren was hoping that the acquisition of Barnes was going to be the final piece of the jigsaw in his quest to take the County Championship away from Yorkshire he was sadly mistaken. Lancashire could finish only fifth in the table with Yorkshire again champions. A combination of the exceptionally bad weather, his knee injury, which caused him to miss five county games, and some indifferent form saw Barnes take only eighty-two championship wickets that season at a cost of twenty-one apiece. Lancashire's other bowlers fared little better, whilst the batting suffered because of the state of Old Trafford's wickets and the weather. Only seven matches were won, five were lost and eleven drawn, the weather being a major factor in the inordinately high number of draws.

With Yorkshire and the weather making the County Championship a procession, 1902 is quite rightly remembered for the visit of the magnificent Australians. The names of most of the 1902 touring team are inextricably linked with the Golden Age. The batting: Trumper, Hill, Darling, Duff, Trumble, Gregory, Noble and the young Warwick Armstrong, who was to have such a wonderful Test career culminating in his leadership of the unbeatable 1921 touring team, was exceptional. And the bowling of Noble, Armstrong, Trumble, Saunders and Jones was a match for the finest of batting teams. Yet the bare statistics of their Test match averages show remarkable inconsistencies. Only Hill and Trumper averaged over thirty with the bat, whilst only Trumble averaged under twenty with the ball. Duff, Darling, Gregory and Noble barely scraped over the hundred-run mark for the series, whilst Ernest Jones, whose reputation as an extremely fast and dangerous bowler should have been enhanced that season, took only three Test match wickets. Compared to England, who had five players averaging over thirty with the bat and three bowlers under twenty with the ball, it is, quite frankly, astonishing that England lost the series.

The truth of the matter is that the 1902 season saw an extraordinary succession of selection blunders. It was the continuation of the Hawke/MacLaren duopoly which had plagued the series of 1899, interfered with the composition of the 1901/2 touring side, and was to reach its nemesis in 1909. Their pathetic machinations make some of the musings of the selection committees of modern times positively comprehensible. Gilbert Jessop puts it succinctly and emphatically in his memoirs: *"It was in the Selection Room that the Rubber was lost."* Once again, to the detriment of the England cricket team, Yorkshire's great patriot and Lancashire's supreme optimist contrived defeat from the jaws of victory.

It is generally regarded, however, that the team that took the field for England in the first two Tests at Birmingham and Lord's was the best combination England has ever selected - and this was without the injured Sydney Barnes. Almost all the first choices from the 1899 team were back in the fold. Fry, Ranjitsinhji and Jackson added flair and skill to the batting, whilst Lockwood, Hirst and Rhodes gave the bowling balance and variety. Add these distinguished cricketers to Maclaren, Tyldesley, Jessop, Braund and wicketkeeper Lilley and what we have is a team with no discernible weaknesses, and that should have been more than capable of giving the Australians a beating on home ground - even without the skills of Sydney Barnes. A measure of the team's obvious batting strength was the fact that Rhodes, at number eleven, was to regularly and successfully open England's batting with Jack Hobbs by the beginning of the next decade.

Things began well for this "dream team" at Birmingham. Thanks to a superb century from Tyldesley, and a stubborn undefeated eighty-one run last wicket partnership from Lockwood and Rhodes, England declared on 376 for nine. Then Rhodes, with a brilliant seven for 17, and Hirst, with three for 15, demolished the Australian batting. Their total of thirty-six all out is still the lowest by either side in an Ashes series. The weather, however, foiled England and MacLaren. When the game finally ended Australia, following on, were 46 for two. A draw was far less than England deserved for their superior cricket. Worse was to come at Lord's, where the weather completely ruined the game. With only two hours play possible England were 102 for two in their first innings - MacLaren and Jackson in full flow - when the game was abandoned as a draw. It was dreadful luck for England, and particularly for MacLaren, who seems to have been constantly dogged by ill-fortune, either through the weather or injuries to key players, throughout his long but unsuccessful reign as England captain.

The series proper, therefore, only got under way at Sheffield on the 3rd July. Not only was this the only Test match ever played in this Yorkshire city, known as the steel capital of the world, but it was also to be Sydney Barnes' only Test match of the summer, and his last until December 1907. By this time the Barnes knee had recovered and he was in good form, so MacLaren felt he was worth risking in a Test match. Two of the dream team were unavailable: Ranjitsinhji and Lockwood. Bobby Abel of Surrey was Ranji's obvious replacement and Barnes seemed an equally logical choice for Lockwood's vacant bowling place. The selectors, however, with Hawke as Chairman, had chosen Yorkshire's Schofield Haigh to replace Lockwood. A spinner replacing a fast bowler was just the first of the comedy of errors executed by Hawke and his fellow selectors that summer. MacLaren, of course, had other ideas. On the morning of the game, seeing the overcast and decidedly poor conditions caused by the excessive number of steel furnaces that existed at that time around Sheffield, he cabled Barnes to turn up and play his first home Test match for England. Barnes arrived - five minutes late - and replaced Haigh on the field. Maclaren's manoeuvre was a complete surprise to Hawke and his fellow selectors - as well as to the massed ranks of Yorkshiremen in the Bramhall Lane terracing.

The crowd, on seeing a Lancastrian replace a Yorkshireman, booed and heckled. Ironically, Hawke was the target of much of the abuse, as shown by one recorded comment from a spectator: *"Here's one of those...selectors,"* screamed the anonymous onlooker, *"And he's a Yorkshireman!"* But it was Sydney Barnes who had to cope with the majority of the crowd's wrath on the field of play. And cope he did, in the only way he knew! Because the game had already begun when Barnes arrived, MacLaren was unable to use him in his favoured position as strike bowler. In fact, Braund had already dismissed Trumper for a single when MacLaren turned to Barnes at the earliest possible opportunity. He quickly rewarded his captain's faith - at the same time silencing the turbulent crowd - by snapping up the next four wickets. Duff, Hill, Darling and Gregory were all dismissed to reduce Australia to 73 for five. Returning later in the innings, he claimed the wickets of Hopkins and Kelly to finish with six for 49 on his home Test debut.

MacLaren was totally vindicated once again. More so when one considers that Hirst, who had performed so admirably at Edgbaston, conceded fifty-nine runs without taking a single wicket and was largely responsible for Australia making as many as 194. England, however, batted badly. From the relatively strong position of 101 for two they subsided to 145 all out. Barnes was less effective second time around, struggling perhaps with his injured knee. His figures were just one for 50, but the wicket was that of Australia's captain Joe Darling, for nought for the second time in the match. It was a dismissal that should have been perceived as a significant psychological blow to the visitors. Hill and Trumper, however, had different ideas and batted superbly, plundering 119 and 62 respectively, leaving England facing a formidable target of 339.

Conditions were now so poor that England stood little chance of victory. The smog hung so thickly over the ground that it could be cut with a knife. Needless to say Sheffield never again hosted a Test match and Barnes' first innings bowling figures have remained in the record books as the best Test bowling on this ground. England managed just 195, of which MacLaren scored 63 and Jessop hit a typically violent 55. It was a devastating defeat which has been put down to the fact that England had the worst of the playing conditions and that only MacLaren of the established cream of English batsmanship played Noble (match figures of eleven for 103) with the requisite degree of caution. Barnes can be absolved from all blame. His match figures of seven for 99 were exceptional considering his indifferent county form and his knee injury. Yet he paid the price with Hawke and his fellow selectors for MacLaren's shocking piece of jiggery-pokery on the morning of the game with his baffling omission from the team to play in the next Test at Old Trafford.

Lord Hawke's memoirs, 'Recollections and Reminiscences', may as well be re-categorised in the fiction section of the British Library. For in it he makes this appeal for continuity:

The ideal would be to play the same team throughout the season. The more this principle is adhered to, the greater the success of the England team. There should be no wanton choppings and changes.

So why Hawke and his fellow selectors, with England one-nil down with two to play, decided to drop Barnes, Fry and Jessop beggars belief. Fry's replacement by Ranjitsinhji after an undistinguished start to the series, collecting just five runs in four innings, was not entirely unexpected. But Jessop had hit a rousing half century in the Sheffield defeat, was a superb cover fieldsman and represented an extra option in the bowling department. He should have been retained. And what of Sydney Barnes? Well, twenty-six wickets, mostly of high calibre Australian batsmen, in three Tests speaks for itself. Even Sydney Smith found his absence hard to fathom:

"The selection of England's team came in for much criticism, more especially regards the omission of Barnes."

It is clear from Hawke's 'Recollections and Reminiscences' that he was either unfit to be an England selector or suffered from such self-delusion that he should have been confined to one of those institutions for the criminally insane which were so fashionable at the time. For he fatuously claims that *"there was never the slightest friction"* between himself, England captains and fellow selectors over policy in his ten years as Chairman of the Selection Committee. As well as angering MacLaren over Rhodes and Hirst's absence from the tour to Australia, he was to upset other captains over selection during the rest of the decade before the spectacular farce of 1909, which led to both Hawke and MacLaren finally being consigned to that graveyard specially reserved for muddled selectors and failed captains. Instead of Fry, Jessop and Barnes, the selectors restored Ranji and Lockwood to a squad of thirteen for the Old Trafford Test, added the stylish but uncapped Lionel Palairet of Somerset and, in a move which was to create a mythology all of its own, chose Fred Tate of Sussex.

The Manchester Test of 1902 has gained notoriety - somewhat unfairly - as "Fred Tate's Match". It was his first and last Test match. How this medium-paced trundler came to replace Sydney Barnes and play such an ill-starred role in one of the most exciting Test matches of all time is a tale of monumental idiocy on the part of both Hawke and MacLaren. On the wet wickets of 1902 he was having the best season of his career. In the County Championship he took 153 wickets, an astonishing total which he never again came near to repeating. The selectors obviously felt he would be effective at Old Trafford if the conditions were right; a reasonable assumption given the notorious Manchester weather. But, as it transpired, the Manchester Test took place in the most pleasant spell of weather of the entire Summer.

The Coronation of Edward VII was about to take place. The whole country was on a high after recovering from the death of the old Queen. Victory on the cricket field over their old Australian enemy was seen as an essential ingredient of that recovery. To the neanderthal meanderings of the Hawke/ MacLaren axis the country came a distant second. With the weather fine Hawke objected to Schofield Haigh as one of the thirteen as, he surmised, Haigh would be twelfth man with Tate discarded from the thirteen. In the absence of Hirst and Rhodes, Hawke needed Haigh for a vital county fixture. Much to the exasperation of Maclaren, Haigh was released. Maclaren, who wanted retain Haigh in case the weather turned on the morning of the game - and seeing Hawke once again usurp his authority as captain - decided to play Tate and make Hirst twelfth man. It was a move deliberately calculated to irritate the Yorkshire supremo.

The match was a classic. Australia won by three runs, retaining the Ashes in the process. Tate was blamed for the defeat, dropping an easy chance from Darling in the second innings - which may have given England an easier target - and being bowled by Saunders with four required to win in the exciting finale. As irony seems to be an extensive feature of Ashes history it is worth mentioning that Fred Tate, on the journey back to Sussex with Ranji after the game, confided: *"I've got a little kid there at home who'll make up for it to me."* Maurice Tate, the aforementioned son, had a long and distinguished career for Sussex and England, including thirty-eight wickets on the 1924/25 tour of Australia, which beat the record that Sydney Barnes was to create in 1911/12 and still stands today. Of all England's bowlers after the end of Sydney Barnes' Test career it was Maurice Tate - son of Fred Tate, the "villain" of Manchester 1902 - who came closest to emulating his amazing feats.

Would Sydney Barnes have made a difference to the outcome at Manchester in 1902? The answer is an unequivocal yes. The game was really won and lost on the first morning when Trumper, with a sumptuous century, Duff (54) and Hill (65) piled on the agony for England's bowlers as they reached 175 for one. It is hard to imagine that Barnes, having dismissed all three cheaply several times in his previous Test matches, would not have made inroads into that Australian innings. It was a staggering piece of selectorial incompetence, especially as Lockwood, similar in style and accuracy to Barnes, had such a productive match, taking eleven wickets for just 76 runs. But, once again, in 'Recollections and Reminiscences', Hawke gives an insight into his rather perverse attitude to the England team when he writes: *"The great point is that it does not matter whether we win or lose, though we should like to win for the sake of England."* He cared little for the success of the England Test team. What mattered to him was Yorkshire. Inadvertently - because of the needs of Yorkshire - he had given Barnes his chance in Australia; deliberately he was to obstruct the Test career of a player who could have single-handedly regained the Ashes for England.

Barnes' name was absent again from the squad for the

final Test at the Oval. This time England won another thrilling encounter by one wicket when Jessop - recalled at last - struck one of the quickest centuries in Test cricket history, Hirst and Rhodes had their famous *"we'll get 'em in singles"* last wicket partnership, and the tension was so unbearable that a spectator devoured the handle of his umbrella. Sydney Barnes' short but sweet Test career seemed to be over, especially as he walked out of county cricket at the end of the 1903 season and was overlooked for the 1903/4 tour to Australia. But Barnes' career at the top level of the game was only just beginning.

4.

BARNES AND THE COUNTY CHAMPIONSHIP

Sydney Barnes' relationship with the County Championship is a unique one. No player has ever represented his country to such devastating effect without at the same time playing first class cricket. A few have appeared for their country from the relative obscurity of minor cricket. For example, Walter Brearley and Cec Parkin, both Lancashire bowlers like Barnes, were occasionally selected for England straight from league cricket. But Barnes is the only player to have played so often under these circumstances. In fact, the Sheffield Test of 1902 was the only time in Sydney Barnes' 27-match Test career that he enjoyed the assumed advantage of being a full-time professional cricketer, playing six days a week and performing on the stage from which England teams have historically been selected. But to Sydney Barnes, as we shall see in the episode that led to his retirement from county cricket, there were no benefits in being a county cricket professional.

As a fledgling fast bowler in the early 1890's Barnes would no doubt have been brought up with tales of the great bowlers of the era. George Lohmann and Bill Lockwood had bowled Surrey to victory in five of the first six official County Championships between 1890 and 1895. Arthur Mold and Johnny Briggs at Lancashire and Bobby Peel at Yorkshire were keeping their respective counties in close contact with their southern rivals. All five were helping England to victories in the Ashes series in England in 1890, 1893 and 1896, and in Australia in 1894/5. Thanks to these five bowlers England were the dominant force in the Test cricket of this period. It would have been the successes of these England bowlers that inspired young men, like the eighteen-year-old Syd Barnes, to take up cricket and reach the top level.

Blessed with a natural bowling action, Barnes made his debut for Warwickshire, as yet not a first class county, in 1893 against Leicestershire, who had also not joined the first class ranks at this stage. Owing to rain he did not bowl a single ball and it was his only appearance of the summer. The following season he played in just two games between August 20th and 24th. The first was against Cheshire, when he had his first bowl for the county. His figures were eight overs, no maidens, no wickets for 27 runs. When added to his eleven runs as a batsman it was very much an undistinguished debut. The second was his first appearance against a first class county. This game was a friendly against none other than the Gloucestershire side of W.G.Grace, Gilbert Jessop and C.L.Townsend.

What is remarkable about this game, other than the fact that Barnes did not bowl a single ball because rain made only three hours play possible in the whole match, was that he is placed on the scorecard as "Mr S.F.Barnes". The "Mr" prefix signified a gentleman amateur. Thus Barnes began his career as a member of an elite to which later he was to prove a thorn in the side. The following year, by now a professional with Rishton in the Lancashire League and known as plain "Barnes", he played in two county games in May, taking nought for 30 and one for 20 against Derbyshire at Birmingham and two for 95 in 33 overs at the Oval against County Champions Surrey, before disappearing for the rest of the season once again.

It was in 1895 that Warwickshire - along with Leicestershire, Hampshire, Essex and Derbyshire - became a first class county. With the expansion of the County Championship one can see the dawn of the Golden Age. There were now more opportunities for gifted young players to play professional cricket, and more chance that the cream would rise to the top. Unfortunately Barnes was not considered as part of that cream. As new entrants to the emerging County Championship Warwickshire would have been trying out as many potential players as possible, inevitably separating the wheat from the chaff. That Barnes was deemed to be the latter rather than the former was a blunder that can be seen in Warwickshire's mid-table mediocrity in the years from 1895 until they finally landed the title in 1911. He played just one more game for them, against Essex at Leyton in the late June of 1896, without taking a single wicket. Thus Sydney Barnes' County Championship career record read three wickets at a cost of 66.33 runs apiece in three matches on his seemingly permanent exit from county cricket.

Of course, Barnes had not performed as well as expected and it was no surprise when he left Warwickshire for Rishton in the Lancashire League. As a level-headed young man in his early twenties he preferred the security of a contract in the burgeoning Lancashire League rather than the vagaries of a professional's life in the expanding County Championship. Rishton made Barnes an offer he could hardly refuse: three pounds and ten shillings a week plus performance bonuses of ten shillings and sixpence for every six-wicket haul and seven and six for every half century. Included in his job description were duties as the groundsman as well as a weekend's cricket. The young Barnes must have been thrilled to be earning so much money for something he loved doing. The average skilled worker still earned not much more than a pound per week, whilst an annual contract with a relatively new county team - like Warwickshire - would have been worth little more than an annual seventy-five pounds. In an average league season Barnes could earn twice as much than with Warwickshire, whilst playing only one or two days a week. It was a lesson in labour economics which he later used to great effect in upsetting the equilibrium of the rulers of the English game.

Over the next few years Sydney Barnes took the Lancashire League by storm, setting records and performing feats which were bound to reach the ears of the county club. It was Albert Neilson Hornby, captain and leading light of Lancashire cricket since 1880, who was the first gentleman amateur to experience what was later to be termed *"the Divine Right of Barnes"* by Neville Cardus. When Hornby attempted to have a look at Barnes by inserting him in a League XI at the expense of a fellow professional immediately before a friendly match at Old Trafford, Barnes - much to Hornby's irritation - objected. It is here that we glimpse Barnes' emergent personality; his sense of self-worth that was to appear time and time again throughout his long career in cricket. He refused to play because he felt that he would be a makeweight on the grounds that he was not originally selected. In the end he agreed to play in a trial match, but his desire to play county cricket evaporated when Hornby suggested he play on the second team. *"I don't wish to boast,"* Barnes is reported to have replied, *"but I think I'm as good as half your first team as it is."*

What Hornby did was to fire the opening shots in a war between Barnes and the establishment which was to last nearly twenty-five years. It was no conventional conflict, but a battle of wills which would ebb and flow with the levels of intransigence of the two combatants. When told how much Barnes was earning in the Lancashire League Hornby had scoffed, remarking that he could get three professionals for that amount of money. Hornby offered Barnes second team cricket in an attempt to put the upstart in his place. Sydney Barnes refused, but had acquired an invaluable early taste of the gentleman at play, whilst Hornby - the archetypal gentleman amateur - was already trying to remind Barnes of his social status. Barnes was never to forget this lesson. It was to stand him in good stead at the end of the 1903 season.

Nevertheless, Lancashire continued to pursue Barnes. He made his debut for the county in 1899, reluctantly and under pressure from Jimmy Sutcliffe, President of the Lancashire League and Burnley, the club to whom Barnes would move the following season. His performance was eye-catching rather than spectacular. His first match was at Brighton against Sussex, when he took just a single wicket for 62 runs off thirty-one overs. Ironically, the Sussex match-winner, who guided them to an innings victory, was none other than Fred Tate, who took nine wickets in the match including six 39 in Lancashire's second innings. For the second time in his five-match county career he then played at the Oval against Surrey. It was the August Bank Holiday Benefit match for the great England fast bowler Tom Richardson. A decent crowd gathered to see Surrey pile up an enormous total of 556. Barnes bowled forty-four overs, fifteen of which were maidens, and took three wickets for 99 runs. As well as demonstrating his capacity for bowling long spells - a trait that was to serve him well in Australia - his stock had risen to such an extent that when he finally accepted that county contract for the 1902 season Lancashire were forced to pay Burnley the princely sum of one hundred pounds for his release. The Lancashire Committee, swayed by the arguments of Archie MacLaren, thought they had the man who would deliver them the County Championship.

The blame for Lancashire's slump from third position in the County Championship of 1901 to fifth in 1902 can hardly be laid on the broad shoulders of Sydney Barnes. His knee injury limited his appearances and effectiveness, yet he still bowled more overs than any other Lancashire bowler and took more wickets. Moreover, he began the season in spectacular style by taking five for 57 against Leicestershire, shooting Yorkshire out for 148 at Sheffield with six for 39, claiming nine Gloucestershire wickets at Bristol and then snatching five for 67 against Somerset at Bath. His knee then gave way and from the 31st May until the 26th June he did not play in any of Lancashire's three fixtures. In fact, he had already missed two games in May because of his knee trouble.

When he returned he performed impressively, taking ten wickets in the match against Surrey at Old Trafford and six against Nottinghamshire at Trent Bridge before producing his six for 49 against Australia in the Sheffield Test. After the Test his productivity declined so dramatically that he took five wickets in an innings only once more in the season, against Gloucestershire at Old Trafford immediately after "Fred Tate's Match", as if to ram home to the selectors their folly in omitting him from the Test side. Had he maintained the form of the first half of the season he would surely have taken more than one hundred wickets. Even so, it seems like a creditable first full season in county cricket. But 1902 was a bowler's year and the top ten in the county averages all claimed their wickets at less than seventeen runs apiece, compared to just Rhodes and Hirst in 1901. Furthermore, the Wisden of 1903 points out that *"there were many days on which he was quite ineffective"* and he was *"only at his best in fits and starts."*

What is exposed in Wisden, from the review of Lancashire's disappointing season and in the cryptic summary of his part in the 1901/2 tour, is the launch of a deliberate campaign by the cricket establishment to denigrate Sydney Barnes' performances for England as exceptional achievements rather than evidence of consistency in order to excuse his absence from the Test team to the press and public. For when Wisden adds such moralistic statements as: *"it cannot be said that he fulfilled the hopes formed of him"* and *"he lacked the perseverance and resolution that would have enabled him to make the most of his natural gifts"* to the comments on his bowling performances, one can sense that the establishment were already perturbed by his behaviour and attitude. The gentlemen amateurs, by accusation and inference, were showing their displeasure at the antics of Barnes the professional player.

The gentleman/player concept that existed in the English cricket world until as late as 1963 was the one fixture that could never be abandoned due to the weather in 1902. The gentleman played for fun; the player for money. For the gentleman not to try when circumstances were against him was acceptable; for the player it was anathema. The player was a paid professional, a mercenary, a worker; the gentleman was an amateur; a philanthropist; an artist. Barnes was aware of the absurdity of this situation and was never afraid to point it out. As Eric Midwinter illuminates, in his Lancashire history 'Red Roses Crest The Caps', Barnes was *"not prepared to bow the knee and touch the forelock"*. Having earned a comfortable living from cricket in the Lancashire League - and knowing that if things did not go his way in the county game he could return - he was always prepared to air his views both on and off the field. He made enemies, particularly amongst the gentlemen amateurs, but also, as John Kay affirms, he *"was never a popular man amongst his fellow professionals"*. To the professional cricketer of the Edwardian age, who saw himself as a typically deferential working man, Barnes' behaviour in negotiating better contracts and berating non-trying gentleman amateurs was seen as discourteous to say the least, whilst his flagrant disregard of the unwritten rule that a gentleman's financial affairs are never discussed piqued the amateur element.

For Sydney Barnes had the best possible tutor in his speedy realisation that gentleman amateurs were the equal of - and not better than - the professional player. His captain for both Lancashire and England was, along with W.G.Grace, the biggest "shamateur" of the age. Archibald Campbell MacLaren, the consummate gentleman amateur, went to Harrow public school then Lancashire County Cricket Club - presumably he was too financially or intellectually challenged for Oxbridge. His father, James MacLaren, was employed as the Lancashire club's Treasurer at the time. MacLaren the professional cricketer was impecunious so often he was given a pseudo-paid position as what was euphemistically described as *"assistant treasurer"* so he could afford to play. When MacLaren's intention to join Hampshire after the 1901 season was announced, the Manchester-based 'Sporting Chronicle', through its anonymous correspondent named as 'Truth', showed just how hypocritical MacLaren's position was with this wonderfully-aimed broadside, appropriately entitled, 'The Future of the Shamateur':

And so MacLaren is to play for Hampshire next season. He has been appointed assistant treasurer of the club. He will be attached to the club house instead of the club ground, as is the ordinary professional. No doubt his experience as assistant treasurer to the Lancashire club will be invaluable. Mr Moberly (of Hampshire), the chairman of the county meeting at which this engagement was announced, did not mince matters. I admire him for his candour. There were, he said, very few first class counties without one or more paid amateurs. That the general effect of such a practice is detrimental to the sport I have no doubt. Above all, any sport, if carried on as a business, should be straightforward and above board. The creation of posts for men who could not otherwise afford to play is a silly subterfuge. Those who hold the posts are professionals pure and simple. They are paid to play as much as any 'pro'. A man is no more nor less of a gentleman, if that is his real social standing, because he takes money for playing. But such a system encourages a class of men who will not exert their abilities to get on in ordinary professional or commercial pursuits. To help to create such a class is a bad thing for the community at large. Such a process tends to make sport, which should be a recreation, occupy too prominent a position in young men's ideas. It will be interesting to see what will happen to these men in the future. They are scarcely likely to become publicans. Without a professional or business training to fall back upon, they are not likely to have the best of times when they become useless as assistant treasurers because they can no longer bat or bowl.

It is an article that could almost have been penned, word-for-word, by Sydney Barnes himself. Moreover, Truth must surely have been some kind of clairvoyant because MacLaren did indeed struggle to make a living outside cricket, with a long series of unsuccessful business ventures. During his early career he was forced to miss the beginning of a season several times due to his commitments as a schoolteacher and his expenses for overseas tours were more often than not in excess of the wages any of the professionals received. In fact, MacLaren was penniless so often his habit of borrowing money, particularly from the professionals in his teams, became legendary. In 1902 and 1903, Barnes would no doubt have been one of those philanthropic professionals, but for the fact that Barnes himself has been famously described as *"mean as they come"*. Barnes' unforgivable sin was to air the apparent contradictions of the disparate social and financial status between the amateur and the professional in his dealings with the relevant authorities - in public as well as private. By the end of the 1903 season the situation came to a predictable conclusion.

1903 proved a much better summer - in cricket terms - for Sydney Barnes, even though Lancashire managed just fourth place in the County Championship. He took 131 wickets at seventeen runs apiece. Only Wilfred Rhodes and Colin Blythe, on the helpful wickets at Leeds and Canterbury, claimed more victims. He was now fully fit and bowled all day on several occasions. Although 1903 was another wet summer batting was easier than in 1902. C.B.Fry averaged over eighty, whilst his Sussex partner Ranjitsinhji managed fifty-eight per innings. Two magnificent performances highlighted Barnes' improved form in the county game. Against Essex at Leyton he took fourteen for 70, whilst at Derby in May he collected the remarkable figures of fourteen for 59. He even had a willing partner in the gentleman amateur Walter Brearley, who claimed 125 wickets in his first full season and was to become a Lancashire legend in his own right. They had the potential to become the most exciting and productive new-ball partnership in the County Championship. Against Surrey at the Oval they claimed all twenty wickets, but all too often the games at Old Trafford were ruined by rain or the wicket was unsuitable for Barnes' style of bowling. Wisden comments, in its 1904 edition, that *"the difference between his best days and his worst was almost immeasurable"*, whilst it again implies a character defect as well as his exceptional skill by pointing out that *"when he was really himself there could be no two opinions as to his quality."*

Being a professional cricketer, and always working to improve his game, Barnes wanted to add to his repertoire and increase his effectiveness in unhelpful conditions. He had absorbed the lessons of the 1902 campaign and decided that he needed a new weapon in his armoury to use on pitches and in conditions that were not receptive to swing and cut. It was during his demolition of Derbyshire that he suddenly discovered his ability to bowl a ball that had never been bowled before - nor successfully imitated since. The leg break, swinging into the batsman then cutting away and rising - delivered at pace - became his shock delivery and would see its use reach its extraordinarily successful climax in South Africa nearly a decade later.

The discovery of this potent weapon, later to be termed

the *'Barnes Ball'* by Neville Cardus, came too late to save his county career. He wanted security, as he had done when he left Warwickshire to become groundsman/professional at Rishton - but Lancashire conspicuously failed to provide it. For, when he demanded a meeting with the Lancashire Secretary and local cotton merchant Sam Swire to discuss terms for the 1904 season, he was not asking for an increase in his weekly wage during the Summer; he was perfectly happy with that. His more than reasonable demands - that the club should find him employment rather than pay him a miserly pound per week during the winter, and that he should have a Benefit match after eight years against the county of his choice - were rejected. The Lancashire Committee felt their pound a week offer was more than generous, whilst the thought of Barnes taking the gate money from the popular Bank Holiday fixture against Yorkshire six years hence was too much for the county's greedy benefactors. In mid-August, on the day after his refusal to sign a contract for the 1904 season, he was dressed and ready to play against Nottinghamshire at Old Trafford when told his services would no longer be required.

This is, perhaps, the dramatic exit that the upper echelons of society - the "gentlemen shamateur" - would have liked to have scripted: unable to bring the working man to heel he is summarily humiliated and dismissed. Even Wisden attempts to write the Barnes obituary:

Before the summer was over, Barnes' connection with the Lancashire Club came to an end. He declined to sign the usual form promising his services for 1904, and in consequence he was left out of the team in the last match. It was stated that he had accepted an offer from the Church Club, and would return to Lancashire League cricket. His defection caused quite a sensation and was commented on in rather bitter terms... Temperament is a great thing in a cricketer, and in this respect Barnes has always been deficient. If he had possessed the enthusiasm for the game that characterised Barlow or Briggs he might have made a great name for himself, his natural gifts as a bowler being so remarkable.

In describing Barnes' departure as a *"defection"* Wisden reveals the true scenario of this affair. Sydney Barnes undoubtedly engineered the whole situation. As an intelligent working man he would have been acutely aware of the perceived master/servant relationship: the master gave the orders unflinchingly; the servant obeyed unceasingly. Barnes knew his temerity in making *"demands"* would end in his being shown the door. He cared little for this petty world of administrators and gentlemen and pined for a return to the leagues, where he was paid more for less work. In county cricket he was an expendable workhorse, who carried the bowling when conditions were with the batsman, but in league cricket he could dictate his own terms and do his own thing. In fact, the only reason that the negotiations lasted as long as they did, and that he did not automatically walk out when his demands were not met, were his respect for MacLaren and Lancashire's lamentable failure to pay him his talent money for the season. Eventually they honoured the debt and reported - rather callously and grudgingly - in the minutes of a Committee meeting on 30th October 1903 that they were *"finally disposing of Barnes"*.

Their hypocrisy, however, is clearly evident just a few months later. In February 1904, following much pleading from Archie MacLaren, they made one last attempt to make him change his mind and sign a contract *"on his merits on the same scale of pay"* as the other Old Trafford professionals. He declined and returned to the Lancashire League. After just fifty games and 226 wickets, at an average of a little under twenty, Barnes' career in county cricket was over.

5.

THE DIVINE RIGHT OF BARNES

It is appropriate at this juncture, and before we examine some of his greatest feats, to take a wider look at the personality of Sydney Francis Barnes. Up to now we have covered a period of less than ten years in his cricket career, and only two of those in any great detail. He lived until 1967, when he was ninety-four years old, and played cricket at an extraordinarily high level until well into his sixties. Although thirty in 1903, an age when most quick bowlers may have seen their better days, his best years still lay before him. He was at the peak of his powers in Test cricket at the age of forty when the First World War could have robbed him of immortality but for the fact that his incredible accomplishments still place him among the celebrated nearly a century later.

In that short space of time we have unearthed not only a great cricketer, but also a remarkable enigma. Benny Green gives an historical perspective to Sydney Barnes by describing him as:

an extraordinary Victorian case, a self-made man whose determination not to be dictated to by committees, nor to be patronised by lesser men, nor to be fobbed off with anything less than what he considered to be just reward for his gifts, smacks more of the latter years of the twentieth century than the fag-end of the nineteenth.

48

A man out of his time is Green's contention. It is undeniably difficult to visualise the era a man is from when he is born during the mid-Victorian England of Disraeli and Gladstone and ended his life with the 1960's of Wilson and Heath. All the improbable events and changes he must have seen in his lifetime: the hot air balloon, the airplane, space travel; the Boer War, the Great War, the Second World War; Victoria, the Abdication, Elizabeth II; a vast expanse of experiences in which Barnes ,in his sphere of influence, played his own distinctive role.

He appeared at Lord's in one other first class game in 1903. Strangely enough it was remarkable for Barnes' batting rather than his bowling. He scored a whirlwind half century but, as a result, was unable to bowl after sustaining yet another injury. A brilliant partnership of 309 between Archie MacLaren and C.B.Fry saved the game for the opposition, although this may never have occurred if Barnes had been able to bowl. The fixture was, ironically, the annual Gentlemen versus Players game. That he played in this social charade - and appeared regularly at the beginning of the next decade - speaks volumes for the character of the man.

As Barnes was asserting himself and his credentials on that cricket field at Lord's - with his supposed betters - other working people were asserting themselves elsewhere. In Manchester, Emily Pankhurst was founding the Women's Social and Political Union, agitating for votes for women. James Keir Hardie was gaining burgeoning support amongst the newly-enfranchised working classes for his Independent Labour Party and its vision of a more equal society. In Hastings, Sussex, a poor house-builder called Robert Tressel was busy writing 'The Ragged-Trousered Philanthropists', a Dickens-inspired novel about a group of Edwardian house-painters at the mercy of their greedy and over-bearing employers, exposing the hypocrisy of the class system and the master/servant relationship of Victoria/Edwardian England. It was a book that was to become a classic of Socialist thinking.

That Barnes should have taken his place at Lord's, in front of one of the largest crowds of the season and in what was seen as the biggest game of this early year of the Edwardian Age, would have seemed perfectly natural to him and not the slightest bit hypocritical. A big occasion demanded the finest and he considered himself - without a shadow of a doubt - part of that elite. He was a master cricketer who felt he deserved the biggest of stages. This goes some way towards explaining his antipathy towards county cricket. Whereas county games were often played in front of sparse crowds, the really big games: Test matches and other representative fixtures, took place in front of full houses.

Moreover, he was acutely aware of what was needed to perform at that highest level. The daily grind of county cricket was no preparation, he surmised, for performing to the limits of one's abilities. So county cricket became a luxury he could afford to do without. His successes between 1907 and 1914 prove this theory beyond doubt. As Pelham Warner was later to observe: *"There can be little doubt that Barnes profits by playing comparatively little cricket, which enables him to keep fresh, and to come to each match full of energy and life."* And Neville Cardus notes accurately the choice that Barnes left the hapless Lancashire administrators: *"it was a case of Lancashire with Barnes, or of England with Barnes."* Naturally, the latter won hands down.

The analogy of the working man fighting for his rightful place in society can be seen throughout his long life. Bernard Hollowood would have learnt a lot about the old master from his contemporaries. He has this to say about Sydney Barnes:

He was a strange man, a social misfit in the cricket scene of

Victorian, Edwardian and Georgian days. He might have been a Keir Hardie or a George Lansbury or a Frank Cousins if he had turned his mind to politics, for he was forever kicking against the pricks and quarrelling with the establishment. He considered himself under-valued by his employers, insufficiently recognised, and overworked, and he would down tools as readily as an East End docker.

It is a portrait of an unusual character for this period, and, despite the forcefulness of his personality, the establishment was always capable of exacting its revenge in the form of not selecting him for the national team. And who could doubt that there were not those amongst the ranks of the professionals who doffed their caps to their amateur "betters" and despised Barnes for his temerity. As Hollowood confirms:

His colleagues admired his skills, but were terrified of incurring his displeasure and found games with him a sore trial. So there was no great outcry when the selectors omitted Barnes from their national elevens. I suspect that on these occasions - and they were numerous - all the more easy-going Players and most of the Gentlemen breathed a sigh of relief. I was frankly afraid of Barnes, afraid of his scowling displeasure, his ferocious glare, his crippling silences and his humiliating verbal scorn, and I played with him and against him only when he was   beginning to mellow!

When H G Owen-Smith of the 1929 South Africans commented: *"He was a funny chap, old S F Barnes"*, it was an absurd under-statement. What we have here is an extraordinary picture of a distinctive individual. Aloof, temperamental, scathing, a larger than life personality who preferred the less rigorous demands of the leagues and minor cricket - and the greater platform of Test cricket and other representative games - to the county circuit. Doubtless had he committed himself to county cricket his records may not have been so impressive. But it was because of his character that he saved himself for those big occasions, fought against petty administrators and made himself the truly great performer he became. When Wisden reported in 1904 that Barnes had little enthusiasm for the game it is palpably incorrect. Nobody tried harder, or worked so tirelessly to improve his skills.

Benny Green exposes Barnes' singular outlook with this perfectly flighted delivery:

It was not that he was immoral but rather that he subscribed to a different morality, that of the artist, who will only give of his best when the circumstances challenge his virtuosity.

Cajoling his team mates and glaring at his own fielders when they made mistakes were in response to a challenge to that *"virtuosity"*. He always gave of his best and when others singularly failed to do the same he was, quite naturally, irked. His superhuman efforts to bowl sides out, usually single-handed, were an expression of supreme skill and determination. When others failed to match his levels of commitment he rebelled. *"There's only one captain,"* he once exclaimed, *"when I'm bowling - Me!"*

Even umpires did not escape his granite-like ferocity. John Kay describes his appeals as *"quiet, but all-demanding"*, whilst Bernard Hollowood recalls that his *"method of registering displeasure at a decision was to stare at the official hard and long, his lean features loaded with disgust and contempt."* He viewed batsmen as some kind of primitive, inferior being: *"His victims were made to feel small"*, writes Kay. As late as 1953, in a tribute to Barnes in The Times, on the occasion of his eightieth birthday, John Hartley gives a convincing indication of his distinctive attitude to the man at the opposite end:

It is only when an incautious word is uttered that one realises that the internal fires are not completely banked down, that age will never entirely mellow this rock of a man. The fateful, kindling word is 'batsmen'. At its sound a frosty look overtakes the bright blue eyes, and a hard edge comes into the Staffordshire accent.

A. N. Other lbw Barnes . . . . o

The Middlesex and England bowler Ian Peebles, in his book 'Batter's Castle', recounts a particularly telling story about Sydney Barnes. The sixty-year-old Barnes had bowled out Sir Julien Cahn's team in a friendly against Staffordshire for eighty. When they batted again it was decided, on the advice of Walter Robins their most experienced player, to try to slog their way out of trouble. Peebles takes up the story:

Walter had come to a powerful decision, and at the start of the next over, abandoning all thought of trying to parry this superb artistry, he rushed down the wicket and let the bat go. In the circumstances it was sheer vandalism, but it worked, and sixteen runs came from the face, edges and back of the bat. This was too much for Barnes who, with the temperament inseparable from genius, snatched his sweater and left the battle to lesser fry

Little wonder then that Neville Cardus called Barnes *"the living image in flannels of the 'Spirit of Denial'"* and, in his 1968 Wisden obituary, described him as having a *"Mephistophelian aspect"*. In later life he freely admitted himself: *"I was a difficult man to play with, I did my best at all times and expected the others to do the same."* One story perhaps illustrates best his singular outlook on the field of play. Staffordshire were playing Lancashire's second XI when Barnes was well into his fifties. The Lancashire side were on the rack with the mercurial Barnes the main tormentor. Most of the fielders were around the bat, including a parson who was only playing as a reward for his services to the county. When Barnes spotted the parson retreating from his position at silly point as he ran in to bowl he stopped suddenly. After a particularly strong verbal admonishment the parson was shown the exact spot on which he should stand. Barnes then delivered a long-hop outside the off stump which the batsman crashed away, missing the terrified parson by inches. No one was in any doubt that the master had given the poor parson a sermon he would never forget.

If his attitude on the field of play reveal a man unprepared to accept second best then his financial dealings reinforce this sense of his own worth. When Barnes made that final break with the county cricket scene we can see that he was not only making the decision for his own peace of mind, but also for financially prudent reasons. At Church he had been offered eight pounds a week plus bonuses, which amounted to more than the annual two hundred pounds that he could expect as a leading Lancashire player. Surely it would have been madness for Barnes to commit himself to hard labour when there was an easier and more rewarding option. Instead of questioning his commitment and motivation Wisden should have been applauding his highly-developed intelligence and his stance as a champion of the rights of the working man, whilst Lancashire should have tried their best to keep such a skilled individual in county cricket by offering him the few hundred pounds which would have secured his services.

But, of course, Wisden was an arm of the establishment - and Lancashire part of that self-same cartel. They would rather suffer the ignominy of defeat on the cricket field than subordinate to the demands of a mere professional. For to make concessions to a strident character like Barnes would have been to open the floodgates to demands from other players. Thus, from 1903 to the end of 1907 he was ostracised by that establishment until, with no other bowler of the requisite standard to turn to, the higher echelons decided they could no longer do without this great iconoclast.

There was another reason why it would have been an act of financial folly for Barnes to continue with his life as a full-time professional cricketer. For he was not the idle professional sportsman of the late 20th Century, enjoying his leisure time drinking and gambling. He had been brought up as the second of five children of Richard Barnes. His father had worked at the same Birmingham firm, Muntz Metal Company, for sixty-three years and would have naturally instilled in his son the ideal of having stable employment with a regular weekly wage. The effect of this working class upbringing cannot be over-emphasised. He saw it as his duty to earn a living at a respectable working man's occupation at all times. Before the First World War he was a clerk at a Staffordshire colliery. After the war he served an apprenticeship as a sign-writer and calligraphist. He worked inscribing illuminated scrolls in the Legal Department of Staffordshire County Council until very near his death. It was a highly-skilled occupation which , just as on the cricket field, he could demand a fair deal for the quality of his work. Ian Peebles gives an insight into his supreme skills as a calligrapher when he describes any letters he received from Barnes as being *"in the most perfect copperplate that any cricketer has ever written, at least in our time."* One of the proudest moments of his life came in 1957 when he presented the Queen with a hand-written scroll he had produced of an account of Queen Elizabeth I's visit to Stafford.

Sydney Barnes, therefore, could afford to menace the establishment. He had no need of their patronage. His skills on and off the field were valuable enough in certain places to maintain a standard of living far in excess of any that the gentlemen of county cricket could offer. It was a fact that he was clearly aware of and exploited to the full. Bernard Hollowood wrote:

His trouble, at root, was that he demanded equality of opportunity and the abolition of class distinctions fifty or sixty years before the rest of the country, and at a time when the lot of the vast majority was docile servitude.

Some evidence exists of a mellowing in later life.

Hollowood alludes to it in the earlier portrait of Barnes' irascible nature. He married before the First World War and the acquisition of a family had an undoubted maturing effect. He became a mentor to several successful players, including Cec Parkin, who performed heroics for Lancashire and England in the years immediately after the Great War, and Jack Ikin, another future Test player, with whom the sixty-one year old Barnes opened the bowling for Staffordshire in 1934 when the young protege was just eighteen years of age. Unusually, he warmly praised a young Yorkshire batsman in 1932. It was none other than the great Len Hutton who, at the tender age of sixteen, had scored an undefeated 69 against Barnes. Hutton himself was later to recall it as *"one of my best innings"*.

Ian Peebles gives, perhaps, the best description of a Barnes in later life who bore little resemblance to the 1903 version. On meeting him at Lord's in 1938, and after mentioning a friendly game that he had organised the following weekend, Peebles recalls Barnes' offer to umpire and to say a few words during the lunch interval. Naturally, Peebles accepted the offer - and was not disappointed when Barnes *"afforded the players the very real courtesy of receiving their efforts as a serious matter demanding his undivided attention"* and produced a marvellous speech to boot.

In the early 1930's he spent some time at Lancashire as the county's bowling coach, charged with spotting native talent and teaching the young players on the staff the fundamentals of his art, a task he performed with skill and diplomacy as well as no little success. Had he been the Barnes of the early 1900's this job may never have come his way. Most astonishing of all was this comment he made about his former Lancashire colleagues, in the committee room as well as on the field: *"If there were more like Mr.Swire and Mr.MacLaren in the game there would be better players and better cricket."* He obviously bore no grudges over the events at the end of the 1903 season.

But there, amongst his ageing acts of civility, are other pieces of evidence which reveal the same man who burst upon the cricket scene in 1901. A favourite anecdote, recounted by many authors, concerns a charity match in the early 1930's when Learie Constantine, established in the Lancashire League as one of the great crowd pleasers of the time, was being beaten time and again by Barnes' guile. *"Chuck 'em up to him, Syd,"* chimed Barnes' captain, sensing the crowd had come to be entertained by some of Constantine's big-hitting. *"I have a reputation as well as Constantine,"* growled Barnes as he angrily snatched his sweater from the umpire. Then Peebles talks of the admonishment he feared from Barnes when a newspaper published a fabricated article under the headline: *"Barnes Tells Young Bowler How To Get Bradman Out"*, following a meeting between the pair.

Another famous Barnes story comes from his retirement days in North Wales when a local builder asked him to appear in a charity game. *"I will do you a favour and play,"* he told the hapless builder, *"if you will do me a favour and build me a house."* Needless to say his absence was assured. Amazingly - and perhaps most revealingly - was the way he had no qualms about using his wife and child as pawns in his dealings with the selectors. To perceive him as a humourless tyrant, however, would be grossly unfair. His laconic humour could always lighten the tensest of situations. For example, having placed a fielder just a yard from the bat and seen the ball drop just inches from his outstretched hand, his cry of *"Save the one, Herbert"* would send both players and spectators into paroxysms of laughter. This tale from Bernard Hollowood illustrates the man as well as any:

He could be an ogre on the field, but away from the business of the day he could relax with pipe and drink sufficiently to be vastly entertaining as he dealt in wry, economic humour, pontificated judgements and mechanical chuckles. At Colwyn Bay, Staffordshire against Denbighshire, a courting couple outside the ground on a rise above the sight-screen distracted a batsman and failed to understand the umpire's yells and gestures. Barnes got up from the grass, where he had been taking a breather, cupped his hands round his mouth and shouted 'Down 'er man! Down 'er!' Then universal laughter, the magic twinkle in Barnes's eye and the 'funny haha' chuckle. Great.

6.

THE BARNES BALL

Whilst the sublime skills of Sydney Barnes were lost to the national and international cricket arenas between 1903 and 1907, the batsmen of the Lancashire League and the Minor Counties Championship were the first to experience the full impact of the new technical innovation he had perfected whilst dismantling Derbyshire in the May of 1903. What were the fundamentals of this unique delivery? Why did it have such an impact on international cricket before the Great War that it immortalised Barnes with the soubriquet "the Barnes Ball"?

To move the ball from the off side to the leg side has always been considered an easier option than moving the ball in the opposite direction. It is a more natural rotation of the arms, wrist and fingers. That is why most bowlers deliver off cutters when they are fast or fast-medium, or off spinners when they are slow or slow-medium. The leg break is a very difficult animal to control and is generally regarded as a more dangerous delivery in terms of dismissing a batsman. The leg break bowler is often expensive due to the difficulty in mastering length and line, but is more likely to pick up a crucial wicket on the grounds that there are more methods of dismissal from a ball turning away from the bat. Even though the leg break had been used effectively by many slow bowlers at the turn of the century, the ability to bowl this ball at some pace was considered impossible. What Barnes developed during his time in the Lancashire League between 1895 and 1901, and his two years in county cricket, reached its ultimate exposition on that spring day in Derby.

He had many advantages, of course, in his endeavours. Blessed with a tall, statuesque gait; a beautiful high action, long and flexible fingers and a mastery of the secrets of length and line, Barnes needed only to convert these basics into the action of the leg break. It was a revolutionary development unprecedented in cricket history. Whereas other developments had their imitators in the years that followed, Barnes' delivery has never been successfully copied.

For the best parallel example we need only look at the innovation of B.J.T.Bosanquet, of Middlesex and England. Bertie Bosanquet - father of Reggie Bosanquet, the famous I.T.N. newsreader of the 1960's and 70's - surfaced in county and international cricket at around the same time as Barnes in the early years of the 20th Century. He was an all-rounder of some repute and helped Middlesex to unseat Yorkshire at the top of the County Championship in 1903. Consequently, he was chosen for the 1903/4 tour of Australia. It was a rise of meteoric proportions which can only be compared with that of Sydney Barnes. Whilst in Australia he succeeded in winning one Test, the fourth at Sydney, with six for 51 in the second innings; a performance that returned the Ashes to England for the first time since 1896. Then, in the summer of 1905, he posted his best Test performance in the first game at Nottingham, eight for 107, which enabled England to go on and retain the Ashes. It was the special delivery he cultivated that delivered England those triumphs.

Throughout the 1890's Bosanquet played a game which he named "Twisti-Twosti". The aim was to deceive the opponent with spin across a table, bouncing and spinning the ball so that his adversary missed it completely. What Bosanquet discovered was that by spinning the ball in a similar way to the leg break he could make it turn in the opposite direction. It was a revolutionary discovery whose ramifications extended over most of the century. One need only look to the successes of Bill O'Reilly, Richie Benaud and, in the modern era, Mushtaq Ahmed, Shane Warne and Anil Kumble for proof of this.

It was in 1900 that Bosanquet first transplanted his hours of practice onto the cricket field. In July, during a county game at Lord's against Leicestershire, he unveiled his new weapon to the cricket world. It had an immediate impact and, as a result, the "googly" was born. Bosanquet's success on the tour to Australia in 1903/4 led to the googly being known there as the "Bosie" - a name it still holds today. Thus, a form of immortality was imposed upon Bosanquet in the same way it was to be given to Barnes. But Bosanquet's invention was soon copied by almost every leg break bowler. On M.C.C.'s tour of South Africa in the winter of 1905/6 the England team - albeit under-strength - were comprehensively destroyed, four Tests to one, by no less than a quartet of Bosanquet imitators in the shape of Schwartz, Faulkner, Vogler and White. Within just a few years of its invention the googly had become an indispensable part of the slow leg break bowler's armoury.

Of all the different types of delivery - from the swing, swerve and cut of the fast and medium-paced bowlers to the leg break, off break, flipper, googly and chinaman of the slower bowlers - the one that the master bowler Sydney Barnes never used was the googly. *"I never needed to!"* countered the offended Barnes in the early 1930's on hearing that the great Don Bradman had espoused the theory that Bill O'Reilly must be a better bowler because he had the googly in his repertoire. And, evidently, he did not. The abundant combinations of delivery he had at his disposal were more than enough for the world's greatest batsmen to handle.

The genesis of Sydney Barnes - from his introduction

to cricket as a callow eighteen year old at his local Smethwick club, to the menacing forty-year-old master of the matting in South Africa - was a lengthy process. When Wisden of 1904 claims that he did not possess *"enthusiasm for the game"* and his *"natural gifts as a bowler"* were *"so remarkable"* it is quite obviously mistaken. He began as a raw fast bowler with a smooth, uncomplicated action. His conspicuous lack of success at Warwickshire saw him re-think his strategy. He decided that pace alone was not enough to trouble the best of batsmen and to achieve the results his pride desired. Instead, he began sacrificing some speed for movement. The Smethwick professional Billy Bird had taught Barnes how to bowl the off break, but it was the ball that moves away that he really wanted to master. He saw this as the delivery which troubled batsmen the most. After long years of hard work and experimentation he finally felt he had succeeded on that May day at Derby in 1903.

Considering the pace that he bowled at, it is little short of remarkable the amount of spin he managed to obtain from the ball. Bernard Hollowood observed that *"mid-on and mid-off could hear the snap of his long fingers as they rolled and squeezed the ball into its revolutionary parabola."* Time and again commentators gasp in awe at the amount of work he was able to induce from a cricket ball; a skill more akin to the slow bowler than the medium or medium/fast. As C.B.Fry, his captain during the Triangular Tournament of 1912, pointed out: *"he had remarkable power of hand, and worked the ball with his fingers at the moment of delivery in a way which is very uncommon with bowlers of more than medium pace."* Neville Cardus describes him evocatively as fingering *"a cricket ball sensitively, like a violinist a fiddle."*

If spin had been the only area that Sydney Barnes practised assiduously then Wisden's comments can be seen as merely gentle untruths. The fact of the matter is that he also tenaciously acquired a mastery of swing and swerve, emphasising the ludicrousness of Wisden's deplorable assessment. In Australia in 1901/2 he spent long hours with Monty Noble, who had so uncharitably upstaged Barnes at the Melbourne Test, learning how to bowl the delivery that swerved to the off and then broke back to the leg. From the left-handed George Hirst the following Summer he absorbed the technique for swerving the ball inwards and breaking it away. Allied to his height - at six feet one he was tall for this period - which made the ball bounce, a rhythmic action and no little speed, he found that in certain conditions he was almost unplayable. *"On a very difficult wicket Barnes, with his tremendous spin, tore pieces out of the turf,"* wrote an awe-struck Pelham Warner after the Gentlemen versus Players match at Lord's in 1909. *"I have never played finer bowling."*

What of his pace? Was he noticeably slower for all his variations? For the answer we need only look to Charles Fry: *"In the matter of pace he may be regarded either as a fast or a fast-medium bowler. He certainly bowled faster some days than others; and on his fastest day was certainly distinctly fast."* The reason why a great player such as Fry found his pace difficult to read was because Barnes gained most of his rapidity off the wicket. *"It is speed off the pitch that counts,"* he was later to insist, because it gave even the greatest batsman no time to adjust to the spin, swing or swerve. What of his accuracy? Did his diversity cause a loss in precision? Warner provides the answer:

He brings the ball down from a great height, he breaks both ways, he keeps a perfect length, and finally his flight is most deceptive. His leg break is not only accurate, but very quick off the pitch. On first going in one is apt to think, judging by the flight of the ball, that it will pitch off the leg-stump, while as a matter of fact eight times out of ten it will pitch on the wicket. This is probably because he bowls from the extreme end of the crease.

BOYS OF OUR EMPIRE

No. 88.—Vol. II. SATURDAY, JUNE 7, 1902. PRICE ONE PENNY.
All Rights Reserved.

Our Champion of the Week.

On the Wicket.

S. F. BARNES,

England's New Fast Bowler.

A FEW months ago there were very few who
had heard of S. F. Barnes, whose name
is now such a household word in connection
with our summer pastime.   This season he is
playing for Lancashire, and his history fur-
nishes another example of how a good man
can be missed.

In the season of 1894, and also that of 1895,
the Warwickshire Executive asked him to
play for them, but only three times in the
two seasons, and it was then rather as a
batsman than as a fast bowler that he went
into the team.

He was born in 1873, and is now twenty-
eight years of age, so that he has plenty of
time for good-class cricket.   He is very tall
(just over six feet in height),   and
knows   how   to   use   every   ounce
of his weight for the game.   For the
last few years he has been engaged in Lancashire League cricket, and the Rishton Club
have had his services as a professional, and
his value may be seen by the fact that in 1897
he made 256 runs, and had an average of 16.
In the next two seasons he had very greatly
improved as a run-getter, and his averages
were 24 and 25 respectively.   In 1900 and
1901 he was engaged for Burnley, and in club
and League cricket his bowling performances
have been perfectly phenomenal.

For some time he has been one of the
most prominent all-round men in the Lancashire League, and very few of those who live
south of Birmingham know what League
cricket means.   There is all the same enthusiasm and excitement as there is about
football—the same large crowds, the same
competition—and the result is that things are
very sprightly.   This kind of cricket, of
course, does a very great deal for the game,
and a large number of cricketers have re-
cruited the county ranks from the various
leagues that are in existence.

In 1897, his third year in the Rishton Club,
Barnes attracted a great deal of notice, and
his bowling average for the year was 8.56 for
81 wickets, a very excellent performance,
which gained for him marked attention.   The
next season was, for him, a still more successful one, since his club won the championship of the League, and this is owing, to a
very large extent, to his bowling, and he took
96 wickets at a cost of 8.44 runs, besides
scoring over a century.

By this time there was no doubt as to his
ability, and in that year his fame began to
spread abroad.   It was about this time that
he tried his luck for the county in the residential qualification, but here again luck
seemed against him so far as first-class

In fact, his use of the crease was not some other clever ploy but purely, he later explained, to obtain a good foothold; something he found essential to his technique. However, guile was also a vital ingredient to his method because, along with his technical prowess, he had limitless powers of analysis, always striving to uncover a batsman's strengths and weaknesses, constantly probing and experimenting in order to turn his bowling into a fine art. Proof of Barnes' great ability to "think out" a batsman is found in the testimony of the great West Indian colossus Learie Constantine, who played against Barnes when the master bowler was over fifty years old.

Constantine's book, 'Cricketer's Carnival', tells the fictional tale of a match between a Contemporaries XI - consisting of such greats as Hobbs, Bradman, Larwood, and Barnes and Constantine themselves, and an Old Timers XI - containing such luminaries as Grace, Trumper, Spofforth and Jessop. Apart from the dazzling compliment Constantine pays Barnes by including him with the *"contemporaries"* against the *"old-timers"* - who to Barnes were every bit as contemporary - Constantine waxes lyrical about the psychology of Sydney Barnes:

Barnes was one of those bowlers whom you never knew how to take. He was over fifty when I first played against him, but he struck me then as the most difficult bowler I have ever had to tackle. He used his head. If you got a four against him, you had an uncomfortable feeling that he gave you that ball and would send down another that looked just the same - but wasn't - and would go up in an easy catch if you made the same stroke. So you went at it gingerly - and then perhaps got caught just the same because Barnes' psychology had foreseen each thought that entered your mind, and bowled accordingly.

Constantine goes on to say that it was Barnes who

taught him the opposite thesis: that when a bowler he found easy to handle was operating it was better to encourage the opposition's captain to persevere with him by playing and missing occasionally. As a youngster Constantine had been reproached by his father for taking apart a bowler called Alonzo to the tune of thirty runs in an over so that his captain was forced to take him off. The great West Indian had ignored his father's criticisms *"until,"* he says, *"in Syd Barnes, I came up against a bowler who used his head to perfection. Suddenly, out there batting, I realised that cricket consists of brains even more than beef".* That great West Indian philosopher, patriot and cricket-lover, C.L.R.James, who was also a friend and compatriot of the Trinidadian Constantine goes, perhaps, to the very essence of Barnes' unique bowling style with this wonderful simile when describing his bowling after he had once dismissed Constantine cheaply: *"After that it was the case of boa constrictor and the rabbits, the only matter of interest being how long he would take to dispose of them."*

The ability to conceal one's intent from the batsman is yet another way the bowler can gain a psychological advantage. And, naturally, Barnes had this ability in abundance. In 'The Cricketer' of March 1978 are some coaching notes he wrote thirty years earlier. *"I want to drive home that the whole run-up action and follow through should be the same,"* he advises on the problem of making the leg and off break indistinguishable. *"The arm should stay at the same height and come over in the same way."*

His wisdom was not always consistent. *"Whatever you do,"* he once exhorted a group of keen young Staffordshire bowlers, *"don't bowl outside the off-stump. Don't wait for the batsman to get himself out - always attack, and always bowl at the stumps." "I never bowled at the wickets,"* he later contradicted in 'The Times'. *"I bowled at the stroke. I intended the batsman to make a stroke, then beat it. I tried to make the batsman move. The time a batsman makes mistakes is when he has to move his feet."*

The latter comment can be put down to a certain haziness of memory in old age because the number of victims he clean bowled or trapped leg before wicket - nearly half of his victims in Test cricket - proves beyond doubt that the stumps were his intended target.

That is not to say that he saw the other ten men as mere appendages to the central battle of ball against bat. He was painstaking in his setting of fields. It was one of the reasons why he aroused such passions amongst spectators. With geometric precision he would move a fielder just a few paces for a particular delivery, and the astonishing thing was the number of times eyewitnesses reported an easy catch resulting from this fastidiousness. For its effect was as much psychological as tactical, especially when the wrath of Barnes fell upon any of his players who dared stray out of position while he was bowling. Bernard Hollowood gives the perfect example of this cunning ploy:

The game had been held up by rain and Staffordshire badly wanted another wicket before the close. The last over was called and the spectators moved to the gates. Barnes was bowling. The batsman defended stubbornly. Five balls were played carefully. Then, in the middle of his long springy run for the last ball, Barnes stopped. He motioned to me at point (two yards from the bat). His long fingers made some sign which I did not understand, but I moved round to silly mid-off. After all, there was only one ball. Once again Barnes turned to bowl, and once again his eyes swept the field as he began his run up to the wicket. I was watching, my hands cupped. His delivery arm was almost over when he halted suddenly, and looked at me with a face as black as thunder. Then, while the crowd laughed derisively, he walked up the pitch and led me (almost by the hand) to the position he had in mind...By this time the poor batsman was in a terrible state. He looked hard at me, and I saw panic in his eyes. Barnes bowled. The batsman prodded forward and the ball popped, so gently into my waiting hands.

His talent was boundless, allying an astute brain to a magnificent technique. Little wonder that he had so much success on the hard wickets of Australia, where an assortment of skills is far more useful than expertise in one particular discipline. The great Australian batsman Charlie Macartney describes - memorably - one delivery during his first Test innings that bowled the majestic Victor Trumper as *"the sort of ball a man might see if he was dreaming or drunk."* It was a talent surely destined for immortality.

The evidence of Ian Peebles provides one of the best descriptions of Barnes' infallible technique. Peebles was a great student of the game and, although he played only a handful of Test matches, was generally regarded as a fine bowler in his own right. In the company of Barnes, however, he drools in admiration:

Barnes gripped the ball firmly between first and third fingers and spun it. Possibly cutters have produced as good a delivery on occasions, but for consistent effect on all surfaces his method has never been equalled. The leg-break was the keystone of the attack, but it was, of course, combined with every refinement of flight, change of pace, life, and accuracy...Barnes' spin was equally potent with an old ball in any weather.

When Peebles met up with Barnes at Lord's in the early 1930's he describes the next hour as *"one of the most entertaining I have ever spent. It was to be expected that one who had raised a fascinating craft to the level of a real art would be worth hearing on the subject"*, he wrote. *"As he talked he demonstrated, wrapping the ball in that wonderfully powerful supple hand, snapping it out and manipulating it like a juggler."* Needless to say, after such a clear enunciation of the Barnes technique Peebles tried, unsuccessfully, to copy it. It was an exceptional method, however, and no one has yet managed to translate the skills involved into effective usage. Now completely enraptured, Peebles is reduced to religious metaphor as Barnes gave an impromptu demonstration:

He ran two or three springy paces, and his sleeve brushed the brim of his hat as his arm came over in a beautiful smooth arc, ending in a supple flip of the wrist. It was the only time I ever saw him bowl, but I had a glimpse of the bowler's promised land.

The last word goes to Bernard Hollowood. His comical book on his life in Staffordshire, 'Cricket on the Brain', contains this amusing passage, which illustrates Barnes' expertise and its inseparability from the man:

My last memory of him will always be of Barnes sitting late at night in the lounge of a Manchester hotel. He is surrounded by young Staffordshire players and we are begging him to reveal some of his secrets. We buy him drinks and he twinkles and chuckles. He rolls a ball in his long fingers and manipulates it like an Epstein fondling a clay bust. The top-spinner like this, see! The leg-break so. The out-swinger, well, hold the ball this way...It is obvious that he considers the demonstration a waste of time. He can tell us what to do, but we couldn't possibly do it. There was only one Barnes.

7.

RETURN OF THE MASTER BOWLER

Sydney Barnes paid for his role in the selection fiascos of 1902, and his acrimonious departure from Old Trafford, with his place in the England team. He was not even considered - never mind selected - for the 1903/4 Tour of Australia. Archie MacLaren, his mentor, was humiliatingly stripped of the England captaincy and, despite his great success as a batsman on previous tours to Australia, was not eager to be a mere foot soldier in a touring party of which he was no longer the leader. Lord Hawke, the initiator of many of England's problems - quite astonishingly - remained in his position as Chairman of Selectors right up to the end of the decade.

Instead, Pelham Warner of Middlesex was appointed as captain. Although this move was heavily criticised at the time on the grounds that he had never played a Test match and was not even the regular captain of his county side, it was a sound decision. Pelham Warner, "Plum" to his closest colleagues, was much more of a diplomat than Archie MacLaren and revealed in Australia an ability to get the best out of his men. He was great friends with all the major personalities of the cricket scene in England and Australia and was later to become a staunch supporter of the skills of Sydney Barnes. His diplomacy was to reach its zenith, incidentally, during the notorious "Bodyline" series of 1932/ 3 when he was the England team manager. Moreover, the selection of Bertie Bosanquet created as big a controversy as that of Sydney Barnes two years previously. Bosanquet, Warner and their colleagues silenced their detractors with the recapture of the Ashes for the first time for nearly a decade.

The first Test at Sydney was won by five wickets, courtesy of a magnificent innings of 287 by debutante R.E.Foster. This was the highest individual innings in a Test until beaten by Don Bradman's 334 at Leeds in 1930, and remains to this day the highest ever innings made on a Test match debut. The second Test in Melbourne saw England victorious by 185 runs. This time it was the bowling of Wilfred Rhodes that won the game. His haul of fifteen wickets for 124 runs eclipsed Sydney Barnes' performance on the same ground in 1902 and was to remain the best Test match bowling figures until Barnes' seventeen wickets against South Africa in Johannesburg in December 1913. Australia rallied in the third Test at Adelaide, winning by 216 runs, thanks to the batting of Trumper, Duff, Hill, Noble and Gregory. But by now Bosanquet was beginning to find his length with the googly. At Adelaide he took seven for 168 in the match, but it was his brilliant six for 51 in the fourth Test at Sydney which brought the Ashes back to England for the first time since 1896. England won that game by 157 runs and although Australia completely dominated the fifth and final Test in Melbourne, winning by 218 runs in a low-scoring game, it was purely as consolation. England had won the series by three games to two.

Wisden pointed out after this tour that *"success was badly needed"*, and it was even more pleasurable for the fact that the team had been given little or no hope on leaving England. The bowling, particularly that of Rhodes, who took thirty-one wickets in the series, but also that of Bosanquet with sixteen victims, Arnold (18), Braund (13) and Hirst (15), had given England a famous victory over this thoroughly magnificent Australian combination. No doubt Lord Hawke and his fellow selectors back in England were giving themselves a well-deserved pat on the back for their consignment of MacLaren and Barnes to the wilderness of Test history. However, MacLaren was to return in glory as a player in 1905 - and as captain in 1909 - whilst Sydney Barnes was to have his moment long after Hawke disappeared to his county in asperity at the end of the decade.

It is worth noting that the performances of Rhodes and Hirst show that, had Hawke made them available for MacLaren's team in 1901/2, England would surely have regained the Ashes two years earlier. No doubt MacLaren felt aggrieved at his sacking as England captain at just the time the strongest England combination was available to tour his beloved Australia. We know that he would dearly have loved to have had another chance to win the Ashes there. But, once again, Hawke had thwarted his ambitions. MacLaren, however, was to gain solace from the 1904 County Championship. His Barnes-less Lancashire team remained undefeated throughout the season, winning sixteen games and drawing ten, to claim the title by a huge margin from Hawke's Yorkshire. It must have provided some consolation to this gifted individual. Sydney Barnes, meanwhile, was gaining comfort of his own through his rapidly expanding wallet. His performances in the Lancashire League and for Staffordshire were earning him amounts of money which the county professional could only dream about, and, whilst he may have regretted not spending another winter in the fine Australian climate, it is certain that he was losing no sleep over the matter.

In 1905 the Australians returned to England. Once again Barnes was overlooked. England were captained, ironically, by Yorkshire's Stanley Jackson. He, too, had little experience of captaincy as at Yorkshire he played under Lord Hawke. Once again it proved an inspirational decision, England beating Australia by two Tests to nil with the other three games drawn heavily in England's favour. This time it was the batting which gave England the edge. No less than six players: Jackson, Fry, Tyldesley, Rhodes, Spooner and the recalled Archie MacLaren averaged over forty. Several bowlers shared the wickets, but it was Bosanquet's superb match-winning eight for 107 in the first Test at Nottingham which set up the England series victory.

These were heady days in England. The Edwardian era, which had begun in a state of anxiety, was now in full bloom and England's success on the cricket field was creating a mood of optimism. Crowds flocked to the Tests and even the defeat by four Tests to one of Plum Warner's weakened England team in South Africa in 1905/6 failed to stem the tide. In any case, that defeat was avenged in 1907 when England, under the captaincy of R.E.Foster, defeated the visiting South Africans and their four-pronged googly attack by one Test to nil in a three-match series. It seemed that the public's appetite for Test cricket, in England, South Africa, but especially in Australia, was insatiable. Neither press nor public called for the reinstatement of Sydney Barnes. But it was this desire for more and more Test matches which ultimately led to Barnes' reincarnation as a Test cricketer.

H S Altham, in his comprehensive 'History of Cricket', describes the touring team that went to Australia in 1907/8 as *"far from representative"* of English cricket. In their clamour for more Test cricket, the press, the public and the game's administrators had forgotten to consult the very men who were central to the game's well-being and the standard of the entertainment provided. For the bulk of England's finest cricketers the tour of Australia in 1907/8 provided a test too far. Of the fifteen men that set out for Australia in the Autumn of 1907 only six had been there before. This heroic sextet were the captain Arthur Jones of Nottinghamshire, Rhodes, Braund, Blythe, Arthur Fielder of Kent and Sydney Barnes.

On the face of it the bowling department seems well catered for. Rhodes had performed exceptionally well on the previous tour, whilst Braund and Blythe had given Barnes sterling support in 1901/2. However, appearances can be deceptive; none more so than the make up of this patchwork squad of players. Wilfred Rhodes' bowling powers were on the wain and, moreover, he was following a path that would eventually lead to his appearance as Jack Hobbs' partner at the top of the England batting order on the 1911/12 tour of Australia. Len Braund had long since seen his best days, whilst Colin Blythe, although still a great bowler, was of such a nervous disposition - particularly in the cauldron of Test cricket - that he fell ill for much of the tour and played in only the first Test at Sydney, taking just one wicket for 88 runs.

Fielder had taken just one Test wicket on the previous tour, but he - along with Barnes - were to be the heroes of this ultimately unsuccessful enterprise: Fielder was to claim twenty-five wickets in the Tests, Barnes was to add twenty-four more victims to his Test aggregate and the pair were to share in the one truly triumphant moment of the whole tour. There was one other notable success in the bowling department, but it was to underline the paucity of skill and experience in this particular tour party. J.N.Crawford, the Surrey all-rounder and a member of a cricket dynasty to rival the Studds and the Fosters, was to top the bowling averages for England in the Tests with thirty wickets at an average of 24.73. But he was the only bowler out of the top ten in the County Championship averages of 1907 to be in Australia. He was soon to part with his county amid much acrimony and ended his playing days in Australia after growing to love the place during this trip.

If the bowling was decidedly thin, the batting was

positively emaciated. Although Jack Hobbs of Surrey and the Nottinghamshire pair of George Gunn and Jack Hardstaff filled the top three places in the Test batting averages, they were all yet to make their debuts before the start of this series. Jones, the captain, had played six Tests but averaged only ten with the bat, but, in any case, was ill for much of the tour and forced to miss the first three Tests, handing over his responsibilities to Fane of Essex. The rest of the batting was almost laughably inept and only Jack Hobbs of the batsmen had finished in the top ten of the previous season's county averages.

It would seem that, with the inclusion of Jones, Hardstaff and Gunn, the selectors were taking too much notice of Nottinghamshire's victory in the 1907 County Championship. Although to an extent this may be true, the fact of the matter was that they were left with little choice. If they had been favouring the men from Nottingham then surely they would have selected Tom Wass and Albert Hallam, who had taken nearly 300 wickets between them in 1907 and thus had been largely responsible for Nottinghamshire's success. The truth of the matter was, though, that Tom "Topsy" Wass and Albert Hallam were working class to the core and considered unsuitable for representative cricket and the obligations that entailed. Compared to Sydney Barnes, the labour aristocrat, they were deemed uncouth and unusable.

The main problem was, of course, that the surfeit of international cricket had taken its toll on England's ageing stars. MacLaren, at thirty-six, had no desire to make a fourth trip to Australia, particularly without the captaincy. Ranjitsinhji was now a prince of Nawanagar in India and would only play county cricket again in 1908 and 1912. Fry, Foster and Spooner were gentlemen who had other calls on their time, whilst Hirst and Tyldesley were in decline and not keen to tour again. Of the bowlers Jessop had more or less finished bowling, Brearley had had a lean 1907 and seemed distracted by constant disagreements with Lancashire, whilst Bosanquet was no longer the shock bowler of 1903/4. No doubt, with one eye on the 1908 County Championship title, Lord Hawke was patriotically unenthusiastic about providing the services of Jackson, Haigh, Hirst and Rhodes, Yorkshire's main bowling quartet, for his country. Thus, when the selectors were casting their net around for a class bowler, experienced in Australian conditions, who would be able to perform to a level which would not mock English cricket, the name they came up with was Sydney Francis Barnes.

Despite his absence from first class cricket since his unceremonious replacement before Lancashire's county game with Nottinghamshire in August 1903, Sydney Barnes had been far from inactive in the years preceding the 1907/8 tour. Playing for Staffordshire as well as in the Lancashire and North Staffordshire Leagues, he had performed feats that minor cricket had never seen before nor experienced since. His record of 119 wickets at an average of 7.83 for Staffordshire in the summer of 1906 is a Minor Counties record that has never been threatened, let alone beaten. For Porthill Park in the North Staffordshire League in 1907, Barnes claimed 112 wickets in only 216 overs at the remarkable average of 3.91. Perhaps Hawke was present at Wakefield in 1907 when Barnes took all ten wickets for just twenty-six runs against a strong Yorkshire Second XI. If he was not, there is little doubt that news of this incredible performance would have soon reached the ears of the Yorkshire and England supremo.

After his reactions years earlier when called into a team through other players' unavailability, Barnes must undoubtedly have been placated by a share of the large profit which was to be made from a Test series in Australia. Full houses at all the venues, with the Australian public urging their team on in their pursuit of the Ashes trophy which they had not held for four years, would have swelled the coffers of the touring England team. Barnes relished, not only the contest of pitting his wits and skill against the likes of Trumper, Hill, Noble, Gregory and Armstrong again, but also the promise of a large cash payment at the end of the tour. In fact, Barnes received a three hundred pound basic payment, a first class ticket for the return sea journey, thirty shillings a week during the sea voyage to cover expenses on board ship and forty shillings a week for expenses whilst in Australia. When added to his wages in the leagues and for Staffordshire it surely made him one of the most financially rewarded professionals in world cricket. It is little wonder then that Barnes was now set to make a place in the England team his own.

Although Barnes' progress around Australia this time was not as spectacular as in 1901/2, he nevertheless proved that his performances then were no flash in the pan. The first two Tests were shared one apiece with two exciting finishes. Australia won the first Test by two wickets, Barnes having his worst match to date. He took just one wicket for 74 in twenty-two overs in the first innings and two for 63 in thirty overs in the second. He renewed his battle with Victor Trumper and the new Australian captain Monty Noble, from whom he had learnt so much on his previous tour, dismissing both fairly cheaply in the second innings.

It was not a disastrous start by any means for this weakened England side, and in the second Test, on what was fast becoming his favourite ground at Melbourne, Barnes' contribution - with the bat as well as the ball - was outstanding. After bowling seventeen wicketless overs for a miserly thirty runs in Australia's first innings, he proceeded to bowl England into a winning position in their second. Five for 72 off 27.4 overs represented Barnes' fifth five-wicket haul in just six Test matches over a period of six years. Set 282 to win the England top order scored steadily and, at 196 for five, looked favourites for victory. However, two wickets fell quickly and Barnes came out to bat with 84 still needed and only three wickets in hand. At 209 he lost Crawford and was joined by Humphries of Derbyshire. The pair added thirty-four before Humphries was leg before to Armstrong for sixteen.

England were now staring defeat in the face. At 243 for nine they were still thirty-nine runs away from victory with just the last pairing of Barnes and Fielder at the wicket. This unlikely match-winning combination edged closer and closer to victory. Barnes struck the winning hit - off the dejected Armstrong - amid scenes of great jubilation from the England camp and their supporters. Wisden points out that *"to the astonishment of everyone"* Barnes and Fielder had won the game. Barnes' contribution was his highest ever Test score, thirty-eight not out. Perhaps Wisden should not have been quite as astonished as it claimed to be. Barnes was no mean batsman - as his performances for Staffordshire were proving - and Fielder was to score 112 not out for Kent in 1909, when he and Frank Woolley were to establish county cricket's best ever tenth wicket partnership of 235 - a record which still stands today.

It seemed as though this victory took too much out of the England team and inspired the Australians to reach superlative heights. For they lost the next two Tests by the convincing margins of 245 runs at Adelaide and 308 runs at Melbourne. Barnes' bowling was steady rather than spectacular: three for 60 and three for 83 at just over two an over in the former game, and one for 37 and one for 69 at under two an over in the latter. His performance with the bat in the second Test had resulted in his promotion up the order, but Barnes was no great batsman and on occasions was known to throw his wicket away; his innings of twelve, eight, three and twenty-two not out bearing testimony to that.

With the series and the Ashes lost, the scene was set for Barnes' finest performance of the tour in the last Test at Sydney. It ended with almost a repeat of his heroics from the second Test. Noble won the toss and batted but Barnes blew away the Australians for 137. His figures were 22.4 overs, six maidens, seven wickets for 60 runs; a phenomenal performance which included the wickets of Trumper, Noble, Macartney, Gregory and Hill. England then scored 281 to lead by 144 runs. But Australia were not about to roll over and die, despite the fact that the series had already been won. Thanks to a brilliant 166 from Trumper, Australia made 422. Barnes could manage only the wicket of O'Connor for 78 runs from twenty-seven overs. Set to score 279 to win England looked to be heading for yet another comprehensive defeat at 57 for five - and again at 87 for six. But Rhodes, with 69, and Jones, at last playing a captain's innings with thirty-four, clawed England back into the game. When Barnes - now at number eleven - joined Crawford eighty-one runs were needed for a seemingly improbable victory. The Australians were beginning to have a distinct feeling of deja-vu as the pair added thirty-one before Saunders finally bowled Barnes for eleven.

Although the series had been lost by four games to one, Sydney Barnes had succeeded in re-establishing himself at the very top level. He had bowled more overs than anyone else in the series, 273.2; delivered more maidens, seventy-four; and had taken twenty-four wickets for 626 runs into the bargain. Even though he finished only third in the England bowling averages it was still a performance of the highest calibre and there is no doubt that he was as respected a cricketer in Australia as any who had gone before. He now had fifty Test wickets at a cost of 20.98, yet his best was still to come.

8.

THE SUMMER OF 1909

When Sydney Barnes returned to England in April of 1908 he celebrated his thirty-fifth birthday. He was at an age when most fast bowlers would be thinking of hanging up their boots. Having played only nine Test matches and two full seasons of county cricket, however, Barnes was still in full control of his faculties and not prone to the staleness which has afflicted many top cricketers over the years. He was essentially a strong and fit man who felt at the peak of his powers and, as photographs of him between now and the Great War prove, he looked a good ten years younger than some of his more junior colleagues.

Furthermore, the selectors had conspired in prolonging his Test match career by making sure he was not over-employed in this standard of cricket. Of the thirty-two Tests, twenty-four against Australia and eight against South Africa, contested between Barnes' debut at Sydney in 1901 to the first Test at Birmingham in 1909, he had played in just nine. For a bowler with fifty wickets in those nine Tests - at a cost of less than twenty-one apiece - it seems, in hindsight, a most unbelievable anomaly. But this tale of selectorial incompetence does not end here. In the Summer of 1909 the selectors, under the unrelentingly amateur leadership of Lord Hawke, were to reach heights of incompetence undreamt of in the aftermath of the Fred Tate incident of 1902.

The first selection mistake of 1909 was the appointment of the captain. Stanley Jackson was the first person asked, by the selection committee of Hawke, C.B.Fry and H.D.G.Leveson Gower, to lead the side. It was a sensible decision given Jackson's successful defence of the Ashes in 1905. Unfortunately, he had to decline the offer due to other commitments, even though many commentators felt he could have been persuaded. A sizeable body of opinion then built up in the media for the reinstatement of Archibald Campbell MacLaren. The Daily Mirror, in an unintentional premonition which even their astrologer could not have contrived to print on its pages without being held up to ridicule, pronounced: *"Players and public alike are clamouring for the return of A.C.MacLaren who is perhaps the greatest captain England ever had though F.S.Jackson is more adept at spinning the coin and winning the toss."*

Not only did MacLaren lose the toss in every game, thus giving credence to the oft-repeated assertion that he was the unluckiest man ever to captain the national side, but also it is doubtful whether he should have been put in that position in the first place. For MacLaren, now no longer captain at Lancashire, was thirty-eight years old and not the force he once was. Since 1895 he had been the scourge of Australia's bowlers, amassing 1,846 runs in thirty Tests at an average in the high thirties. During the 1909 series he was to see his reputation as a master performer of the Golden Age tarnished by managing just eighty-five runs in seven innings with an average barely above twelve.

Of course, this was not the only reason why his appointment should not have been countenanced. Evidently, short memories were at work in the world of cricket, because the combination of Hawke as Chairman of Selectors and MacLaren as captain was as sure to create chaos and confusion as it had done in 1902. Their mutual enmity could not have subsided to such a degree by 1909 that they would now make an effective partnership and win back the Ashes.

Plum Warner gives, perhaps, the best description of why the appointment of MacLaren was certain to prove calamitous:

There can be no doubt that a mistake was made in asking MacLaren to be Captain, for that once grand cricketer was now a long way past his best both as a batsman and a fieldsman; and he did not get on with his selectors or they with him.

The selectors, with a faux pas of extraordinary stupidity, had relinquished the series before it had even started. The mistake was to bow to the pressure to choose MacLaren to captain the team. Because of his undoubtedly strong and forthright personality - and his imperious manner at the crease - MacLaren had made himself a popular hero amongst cricket players, cricket watchers and cricket writers alike. One need only see how successfully he got the best out of Sydney Barnes, with his mood swings and temperamental behaviour, to perceive that MacLaren was a man of infinite charm. He was very much a popular hero in the typically British mould of the gallant - but unlucky - loser. This is maybe why incidents in British history, such as the Charge of the Light Brigade and the evacuation of Dunkirk are seen as glorious failures. MacLaren was seen as the man to make the last ditch stand in the face of adversity, even if it did mean another lamentable flop. Allen Synge, with the requisite degree of humour and gravitas, describes the situation thus in 'Sins of Omission', his chronicle of the mistakes made by the England selectors between 1899 and 1989:

Evidently Hawke bowed to public opinion in 1909, or perhaps to some higher power that decreed that this cantankerous and diverse pair should forever be shackled together in misfortune for England, like two argumentative characters in an over-long play by Samuel Beckett.

It seems astounding that Hawke should sanction such a retrograde step considering the compelling evidence of history. C.B.Fry, in his memoirs, paints a picture of Hawke as not the natural incompetent we have seen so far, but as a weak leader, easily influenced by the prejudices of others. Fry describes Hawke as *"much too observant of what he thought was public opinion. He was much misrepresented as the strong man of cricket."* So if Hawke was a weak leader and Fry, as he seems to suggest by his comments, was against MacLaren's candidature, who was the third member of the selection panel who must have voted for the Lancastrian pessimist?

H.D.G.Leveson Gower, a reasonable cricketer in his own right and captain of one of the less successful Surrey teams during this decade, was an eccentric bordering on lunacy. This colourful scion of the Golden Age reputedly bit the arm of the Governor of British Guinea in 1897 for a bet! When the 1945-50 Labour Government's nationalisation programme was in full swing he is said to have loudly entreated Prime Minister Clement Attlee to *"play a straight bat!"* and cancel the policy from his box at Lord's. He was clearly in awe of MacLaren. In his autobiography, 'Off and On the Field', he claims to have been responsible for Jack Hobbs' first appearance for his country in England for the first Test at Birmingham in 1909 - against the captain's advice. When Hobbs was out for a duck in his first innings he recalls, fearfully: *"I imagined MacLaren's eye one me!"* Naturally, Leveson Gower would have been suitably gratified by Hobbs' 62 not out in the second innings of that first Test, enabling England to win by ten wickets. However, Hawke, MacLaren and Leveson Gower were now about to preside over some of the most astonishing selection blunders of all time.

Though the series began well for England, it did not for Sydney Barnes. With his record against Australia already marking him out as one of the Ashes greats, it seems the height of folly that he was omitted from the first two games. With MacLaren as captain, it seems doubly mystifying that he did not take the field at Birmingham, whilst the Wisden of 1910 says he *"should have been picked for all five matches."* Maybe he was already considered too old, but as MacLaren himself was two years older than Barnes this is an unlikely explanation. Plum Warner merely comments: *"Barnes, the best bowler in England, was, it seemed, not considered"*, whilst the Daily Express was equally perplexed when it stated *"that no one knows whether Barnes was invited or not."* Sydney Barnes was apparently still not a favourite with the status quo.

If the press, public and players of England were amazed at the omission of Barnes for the first two Tests then the Australians were equally as shocked. Charlie Macartney, embarking on a long and successful Test career at this time, wrote, in his biography 'My Cricketing Days':

One of the outstanding omissions of the 1909 season on England's part was that of Barnes. He played in three of the five Tests that year, but had he been in the whole series it might have made all the difference. He was the best bowler England produced in his time, and he is the best bowler I have met on all wickets home and abroad. Tate, for instance, is a better bowler in Australia than in England, and Foster was the same. Blythe, Rhodes and Hirst were better in England than in Australia, but Barnes was top class on all wickets.

Unfortunately for Barnes, MacLaren was no longer accorded something of the carte blanche approach in selection matters that had been the case in the late 1890's and early 1900's. His record before the 1909 series, captain on seventeen occasions whilst losing nine and winning only three Tests, was not that of the most successful captain England have ever had. Moreover, he had captained in four series without ever winning the Ashes. His stock had fallen to such an extent that he would have been unable to secure a place for Sydney

Barnes, even though he was the one unqualified success of his previous reign as England captain.

Having been disregarded for England's first Test victory, Barnes was overlooked once again for the Lord's disaster. He was not the only one. The Daily Express explained: *"Neither luck nor the Australians won the Test match, but the English selection committee who picked out absolutely the most irrepresentative side that has ever taken the field in this country,"* whilst 'Bailey's Magazine' suggested the Selection Committee had *"betrayed England to Australia."* From the winning team at Birmingham only MacLaren, Hobbs, Tyldesley, Jones, Hirst and Lilley survived. Fry was involved in a law suit and was unavailable - as a selector as well as a player. Blythe, whose eleven wickets had won the first Test, was suffering from his recurring nervous disorder and was under doctor's orders not to play either. The Northants fast bowler, G.J.Thompson, saw his Test career terminated after one Test and just four overs. Incredibly, Jessop and Rhodes also suffered the selectors' axe. In their places came an injured Tom Hayward, the inexperienced George Gunn, the Leicester all-rounder J.H.King for his one and only Test, and the bowlers Schofield Haigh and A.E.Relf, with just five Test wickets between them, for their third and last internationals against the Australians.

Because of the nature of the Lord's wicket most respected observers felt that a fast bowler was needed to exploit the conditions. Apart from the obvious option of Sydney Barnes, the most successful bowler in England at the time was Walter Brearley, Barnes' old sparring partner at Lancashire. As luck would have it, Brearley was at Lord's on the first morning of the second Test. MacLaren attempted - at a quarter past eleven - to persuade Brearley to play in the game. It was a mirror image of the Sheffield debacle of 1902, when Sydney Barnes was the last minute selection. But this time MacLaren failed because Brearley's kit was already on its way to Tonbridge for a county game. Brearley would dearly have loved to play, as shown by his subsequent display of petulance in front of Leveson Gower, who, with Fry in court and Hawke at the spa resort of Aix-les-Bains in France *"for health reasons"*, was the only selector available for anyone to blame for the sad state of affairs. The uncompromising Brearley had to be moved on by the police as he loudly castigated the selectors for their errors.

England lost the Test by nine wickets, a brilliant undefeated century by Ransford and six for 35 from Armstrong in England's second innings being mainly responsible. MacLaren offered to resign but, with the series all square, the selectors felt there was - as yet - no cause for alarm. The team for the third Test at Leeds was a much better balanced side. Back came Fry, Rhodes, Jessop and Brearley, Jack Sharp, the Lancashire all-rounder and Everton footballer was chosen to make his Test debut, and - at long last - Sydney Barnes. It seemed that all was well again. But England suffered the loss of Jessop after just an hour of the game when he strained his back so badly in the field that he did not play again that season, and the batting failed in the second innings on a wet wicket. The Australian heroes were the fast bowler Tibby Cotter, who took five for 38 in England's second innings' 87 all out, and the young Charlie Macartney, with eleven wickets in the match at a cost of 85 runs.

Sydney Barnes had a superb game and sealed his place for the rest of the series. In Australia's first innings he took just one wicket - that of top scorer Syd Gregory - for 37 runs in twenty-five overs. Despite his lack of wickets there is no doubt that his economical bowling put pressure on the Australians, enabling Rhodes, Brearley and Hirst to reap the rewards. The second innings was a different story. He took five of the first six wickets to fall - including Victor Trumper for two - to help reduce Australia to 127 for seven and give England a chance of victory. The Australians rallied, however, eventually raising their score to 207. Barnes' figures were thirty-five overs, eighteen of them maidens, six wickets for 63 runs. It was a magnificent piece of bowling and the seventh time in ten Test matches that Barnes had taken five wickets or more in an innings.

Australia now led two-one in the series and that was the way it was to remain. At Manchester rain intervened and the game was drawn after another woeful England batting performance. Once again Sydney Barnes bowled England into a good position. With five for 56 from twenty-seven overs he had been instrumental in bowling Australia all out for 147. He dismissed Bardsley, Ransford, Trumper - who must surely have been sick of the sight of Barnes by now - Macartney and Carter cheaply. England's inept batting, and the destructive bowling of Frank Laver, who took eight for 31, left them with a twenty-eight run deficit. By his own standards Barnes' bowling went a little awry in Australia's second innings. He went for 66 runs in 22.3 overs, the wicket of Carter being his only success. The game ended with England on 108 for three, 200 runs short of victory. The final Test was a more high-scoring affair, but when the game ended the situation was almost exactly the same as at Old Trafford: England 104 for three, needing another 209 for victory. Barnes was less successful in this game, bowling forty-six overs and taking four wickets for 118 runs in the match. Nevertheless, it was still a performance of the highest calibre on the marvellous Oval batting wicket.

What is surprising is not Barnes' economical and productive bowling, but the fact that he played in all those last three Tests at all. Given the selectors' constant misuse of his services, and the maelstrom of choppings and changes after the Lords' debacle, it would have been no surprise to see Barnes dropped again in spite of his successes. For, after Australia went two-one up with two to play at Leeds - against probably England's best eleven of the Summer - Hawke and

Leveson Gower conspired to make four changes for the Manchester Test and then four more at the Oval. During the series the selectors chose no less than twenty-five different players, a figure only exceeded in 1921 and 1989. In 1921 twenty-nine players were chosen, but there was at least some sort of excuse in that England were still in disarray after the losses of the Great War. Of the twenty-five chosen in 1909 no less than sixteen: Sharp, Hayes, Hutchings, Relf, Jones, Hirst, Haigh, Carr, Thompson, Blythe, Jessop, Brearley, Hayward, Tyldesley, King and MacLaren never played against the Australians in a Test match again.

Although Leveson Gower was to appear on selection committees after the Great War, Lord Hawke was finally dispatched to the selectors' graveyard. Charles Fry was to be the only remnant left of the 1909 fiasco when made captain for the whole of the 1912 Triangular Tournament. He had been the one calming influence during this troubled season and had constantly balked at the antics of MacLaren, Hawke and Leveson Gower. When, in his memoirs, he says: *"I have not much good to say of our meetings,"* he reflects the total sense of bewilderment that the English cricket world had felt with the selections of 1909. Barnes, on the other hand, had suffered enough to the vagaries of Hawke and the misplaced patronage of Archie MacLaren over the previous eight years. He had performed so splendidly that he was now - at last - to become a permanent fixture in the England team. In three Tests he had taken seventeen wickets at exactly twenty runs apiece. His Test match aggregate was now sixty-seven wickets at an average of 20.73. Having played in just nine out of thirty-four Tests since his debut in 1901, he was now to embark on a sequence of eighteen Test appearances for England, missing only the 1909/10 trip to South Africa by a weak England team.

In the Wisden of 1910 he was awarded the ultimate accolade and named as one of the 'Five Cricketers of the Year'.

Having more or less written his obituary in the 1904 edition, Wisden was now having to revise some of its previously anodyne opinions: *"The disagreement that caused him to drop out of the eleven was an even greater misfortune to Lancashire than the player himself"*, it magnanimously asserts of his split with the red rose county seven years earlier. He had finally gained the respect of the establishment - a respect that he had always sought but never craved - as much for his rejuvenation of Staffordshire cricket as his performances in Australia in 1907/8 and in the final three Tests of 1909. In the Gentlemen versus Players game at Lord's in 1909 he had played a leading role in the professionals' 200-run victory by taking five wickets, including a hat-trick, for 22 in sixteen overs in the first innings and three for 33 off twenty-one overs in the second. Plum Warner, who toiled against Barnes for the gentlemen's top score in the game, paid him this glowing tribute in the same Wisden portrait, emphasising the esteem in which he was now held:

Barnes certainly did not bowl one bad ball during the two innings of the Gentlemen, and a finer bowler I have never played, and in saying this I do not forget Lockwood or Trumble, or the best of the South African bowlers...I had only seen Barnes bowl once before, and that was in a Middlesex and Lancashire match at Lord's, six years ago, but I remember Mr. Clement Hill telling me that Barnes was the best bowler he had ever played on an Australian wicket. Certainly he is the best bowler in England today.

9.

MELBOURNE MARVEL

If Barnes' accomplishments so far in his Test career had marked him out as a truly great bowler, his subsequent feats on the Australian tour of 1911/12, during the Triangular Tournament of 1912 and in South Africa in 1913/14 were to establish him, arguably, as the greatest practitioner of all time. His strike rate up to and including the 1909 series was as good as any of the great bowlers who were either his contemporaries or predecessors. Peel, Briggs, Lohmann and Richardson for England, and Turner, Spofforth, Trumble and Noble of Australia all had comparable records at this point in Test history. However, in the two years between December 1911 and January of 1914 Barnes was to eclipse all Test records.

What is most surprising, perhaps, is that he created these records at an extraordinary age. When he left for Australia with the England tour party in October 1911 he was already thirty-eight years old, and when he played his last Test in South Africa in January 1914 he was almost forty-one. Although several players have been selected for their countries at a more advanced age - some in their fifties - none have produced such record-breaking performances. Instead of declining with age, Barnes - like a fine wine - had matured into a master bowler. The gentlemen in the corridors of power at Lord's were beginning to understand that Sydney Barnes was an invaluable asset to any England side and could no longer be disregarded, despite his preference for league and minor counties cricket. It is no surprise that when the M.C.C. chose their touring party for Australia at the end of the 1911 season Sydney Barnes' name was the first on the list.

Through a combination of selectorial incompetence, bad luck and the excellence of the Australians, England had won just two series out of eight against the old enemy since 1896. It was a disappointing record, especially considering the depth of talent that was at its disposal. It is tempting to regard Sydney Barnes as a cause rather than a symptom of England's failures. He had taken part in four of those series - all of which had been lost - whilst of the twelve Tests in which he had appeared only two had been won, compared to eight defeats and two draws. It was an unenviable record. If many observers felt he was unlucky - or even a jinx - it is certain that he would not have felt that way. Sydney Barnes had little truck with luck. He was a professional performing to the limits of his ability and, over the next two years, he was about to prove it as England were to win twelve Tests, drawing two because of the weather, and losing just a solitary match. That defeat was to take place in the first Test of the 1911/12 tour, thus ensuring that many commentators feared the continuation of England's cycle of disaster and under-achievement. For this tour had already begun in inauspicious circumstances.

As already evidenced, the 1909 series had seen the end of many players' Test careers. It was something of a transitional period and, of the sixteen-man squad that left for Australia in the Autumn of 1911, only Barnes, Warner, Rhodes, Hobbs and Gunn had been there before. Furthermore, only Warner and Rhodes had experience of a winning Ashes series. It seemed that the selectors had made the same mistake as for the 1907/8 tour by including three members of the 1911 county champions Warwickshire, a team for whom Sydney Barnes could have been playing had circumstances been different. Septimus Paul Kinnear had been selected largely on the strength of an innings of 268 not out against a weak Hampshire bowling attack at Edgbaston, and, indeed, his only Test was to be the defeat in the first game at Sydney. His county colleague, the wicketkeeper E.J. "Tiger" Smith, played in four of the Tests in Australia and during the Triangular Tournament in 1912, but only after Herbert Strudwick, who was later to have a long and successful Test career, had been made one of the scapegoats for the first Test defeat on his debut. The third Warwickshire player, however, was to have a tremendous influence not only on the destination of the Ashes, but also on the form and well-being of Sydney Barnes.

Frank Foster, the Warwickshire amateur captain and all-rounder, enjoyed a marvellous season in 1911. He had performed the double, scoring 1,383 runs at an average of 44.61 and taking 116 wickets at less than twenty apiece, and captained his county with skill and assurance. Although supremely gifted, he had fulfilled less than what had been expected of him since his debut in 1908. Between April 1911 and March 1912, however, he was to have an annus mirabilis and, along with Sydney Barnes, was to form the most successful opening attack England have ever sent to Australia.

The third seam bowler, and one of only three gentlemen amateurs in the tour party with Foster and Warner, was the Essex captain and all-rounder J.W.H.T.Douglas. Before the first Test at Sydney neither Foster nor Douglas had made their Test debuts. None of the rest of the squad had any Test match experience except Frank Woolley, who had played in just one Test in the 1909 debacle. In fact, of the players that arrived in Australia in November 1911 only Barnes, Rhodes, Hobbs, Foster, Douglas and Woolley - along with Strudwick - were to have much more of a Test career. But it was the brilliance of this sextet which gave England their most convincing victory ever on Australian soil.

Inevitably, the team's lack of experience led to it being subjected to the usual criticism and abuse by the Press. Some of the top performers of the 1911 season had been overlooked. Whilst Fry and Spooner were unavailable, the experienced Tom Hayward had returned to something like his glorious best with nearly 2,000 runs. Jack Hardstaff had reaped a harvest of runs too. The country's top wicket-taker was Lancashire's Harry Dean, and G.J.Thompson had also excelled enough to warrant his inclusion in the touring party. All four were mysteriously ignored. The choice of Plum Warner as captain, however, did not provoke the same amount of criticism. He had proved an excellent leader of men on the successful 1903/4 tour, but he was only the second choice to captain the side. C.B.Fry had originally been asked to lead but was unable to spare the time. Moreover, confusion reigned in the England camp when Warner fell seriously ill at the beginning of the tour with a ruptured duodenal ulcer and was unable to play at all in the series. With only two other amateurs in the squad, and, of course, an amateur captain still regarded by the establishment as the only way to retain the social order, the mantle of captaincy fell on Johnnie Douglas.

It is of no little incidental amusement that Douglas was nicknamed *"Johnnie Won't Hit Today"*. The captain of Essex was the archetypal gentleman amateur, leading Essex to outstanding feats of mediocrity as well as being an accomplished amateur boxer of the Queensberry variety, winning a Gold Medal at the London Olympics in 1908. He was the type of gentleman captain whose decision whether to bat or bowl on the morning of a game was not based on any scientific analysis of the wicket, nor on the relative strengths and weaknesses of the opposition, but rather on his own predilection either to hit a few balls or to turn his arm over a few times. Sydney Barnes, as one of the most experienced players on the team, was soon to disabuse him of this preposterously amateur notion. For, when Douglas led out the England team for his first Test match on that sunny Sydney morning on December 15th 1911, he decided - much to the horror and amazement of Sydney Barnes - to partner his fellow amateur Frank Foster in England's new ball attack. Barnes' riposte was to give Douglas his first lesson in the Divine Right of Barnes: *"That's all very well, Mr Douglas, but what am I 'ere for?"*

If any of Barnes' quotes can be said to sum up the man it is this ostensibly quizzical remark. Sydney Barnes, the experienced professional, was nonplussed by his captain's lack of grasp of the obvious: that he, the master bowler, was the only player capable of using that new ball with the ultimate goal of winning the Ashes. And he was unafraid to tell his supposed better this self-evident truth. When one looks at old photographs of that 1911/12 touring team one sees a different Sydney Barnes from those of the early 1900's, when he was a regular county cricketer with Lancashire. Gone is the fierce moustache and the permanent scowl, a product no doubt of the under-paid and cynical professional cricketer's life. Instead, it is a relaxed glare; arms and legs folded, right over left. He is seated at the end of the front row alongside his colleague and equal Wilfred Rhodes - previously the sole preserve of the gentleman amateur. It is a confident pose; the pose of man who knows his rightful place in society; the bearing of the newly-enfranchised and represented labour aristocracy: a great man at peace with a world in which he was a first among equals.

Naturally, Douglas's decision to open with himself instead of Barnes on that first morning of the series in Sydney was an unmitigated disaster. Hill, Armstrong and - with a glorious century - the incomparable Victor Trumper combined to wrest the initiative in Australia's favour. Even though Barnes was England's best bowler in the innings, with three for 107 from thirty-five overs, he could not prevent

Australia from piling up 447 runs. England's batting was consistent in both innings, but the damage had already been done. Faced with a huge target of 438 in their second innings, England were bowled out for 291. H.V.Hordern, on his Test debut, had the superb match figures of twelve for 175. It was not until Bob Massie swung his way to sixteen wickets at Lord's in 1972 that this debut bowling performance was bettered. In Australia's second innings Barnes took one for 72 from thirty overs, whilst Foster, with five for 92, made a splendid entry into Test cricket.

Sydney Barnes had made an unremarkable start to the series. Statistically-speaking, it was England's worst ever first Test performance in Australia in the history of Ashes cricket. To the public back in England the team was in disarray and driving headlong into yet another calamity. Do not forget that 1912 was to be the year of the catastrophe: In January, Captain Robert Falcon Scott and his companions were to die in a blizzard in their gloriously unsuccessful attempt at being the first to the South Pole, whilst in April the "unsinkable" S.S.Titanic was to find its watery grave off the coast of Newfoundland with the loss of 1,513 lives. The defeat of England's cricketers in Sydney was every bit as damaging to the national psyche as these two disasters were to become.

That this England side was to fly in the face of history and portent was not the miracle some commentators were no doubt praying for, but an amalgamation of the talents of the English professional - as epitomised by Barnes, Rhodes, Hobbs and Woolley - and the leadership and common sense of the gentleman amateur, in the shape of Douglas and Foster. For Douglas, after an acrimonious meeting with the more experienced members of his team, made two crucial tactical changes. The first was the most obvious and already alluded to by Sydney Barnes. From the second Test onwards Barnes was to share the new ball with Foster and Douglas was to never again supplant him as a Test match opening bowler.

Secondly, Wilfred Rhodes was to complete his odyssey up the England batting order by now becoming Jack Hobbs' regular opening partner. It was to become one of England's most productive ever partnerships.

These changes were to have an immediate and spectacular impact on the opening day of the second Test in Melbourne. The Melbourne Cricket Ground had become, by dint of his performances there, Sydney Barnes' favourite venue. But nothing before or after in Barnes' exceptional career can match what he did on that Melbourne morning on the 30th December 1911. Sydney Smith probably understates Barnes' performance when he describes him as being a *"destroying angel"*. For Barnes, in a bowling spell of unremitting hostility, captured five wickets for a mere six runs in eleven overs, seven of which were maidens. It was the turning point of the whole series. Let Plum Warner, watching from his sick-bed in the England dressing-room, set the scene:

A somewhat cold, unsettled-looking morning, with occasional light showers. Hill wins the toss.... There was a beautiful wicket: the drizzle had rendered the ball just a wee bit slippery, and perhaps had taken the pace from the pitch. Foster opened the attack, and Barnes bowled from the railway end. One heard on all sides that Australia would make a big score. Foster bowls a maiden to Kelleway, then Barnes takes the ball. Tall, upright, broad and fit-looking, he is full of life as he runs up to the wicket. A few steps, then a couple of strides with both feet off the ground together, and the ball is delivered with concentration and marked energy.

Barnes completely shattered the morale and assurance of Australia's frontline batting to such an extent that it never really recovered until after the First World War. To begin with he bowled Bardsley off his pads for nought. The great Clem Hill then followed, bowled by a beautiful in-swinging yorker.

An appeal for leg before against Kelleway was upheld, followed by Armstrong, caught at the wicket. Australia were now 11 for four and in a state of total panic, and, as Warner testifies, *"paralysed"* when Barnes was bowling. The next Barnes over began with an uncharacteristic high full toss. Incredibly, he had almost missed this Test match and his greatest triumph because of illness. He complained to Douglas that everything seemed to be going round and round and that he couldn't see the batsman at the other end. To the obvious pleasure of the crowd - and the relief of the Australian batsmen - he left the field, not to return until after lunch. Trumper and Ransford edged the score along to thirty-two, amidst a break for rain, before the interval. Immediately after lunch Foster bowled Trumper for thirteen. Five runs later Barnes had Minnett caught by Hobbs in the covers to leave the Australians staring humiliation in the face at 38 for six. Barnes' figures were an unbelievable five for six. Moreover, the balls that didn't take wickets reared and struck the batsmen with alarming regularity. As Clem Hill was later to testify: *"Some of us carried blue and yellow bruises on our thighs for days. He made them come faster from the pitch than Foster did and Foster was faster through the air!"* It was the most destructive piece of bowling in Test cricket history.

Barnes took no more wickets in the innings but displayed the petulant side to his nature. With the score at 125 for eight he was brought on to try to finish off the Australians. A section of the crowd began barracking him when he took his time to set a field. Although it was a sign that Barnes and England were on top, he proceeded to throw the ball down and fold his arms, refusing to deliver the next ball until the barracking had stopped. It was a gesture that only Barnes amongst his illustrious contemporaries was able to get away with. In fact, most Australian commentators found the behaviour of a small section of the crowd reprehensible. One Sydney critic wrote:

It was a most unwarranted display against a man who had bowled magnificently. It evidenced, too, a most partisan spirit. It was confined to a hostile section in the shilling stand, and such unfair treatment undoubtedly interfered with Barnes's bowling. In the next over there was a similar outbreak by the hoodlums, but the occupants of the members' reserve cheered him and the noisy element was quickly quelled by the counter-demonstration.

To their credit, Australia rallied. Ransford (43), Hordern (49 not out) and Carter (29) enabled them to reach 184 before finally being dismissed. Barnes took no more wickets, but the memory of his display was to haunt them for the rest of the series. He had blown away the best Australia could offer as if he had been mopping up the tail-enders on a Saturday afternoon in his beloved North Staffordshire League. Only Trumper of the great Australian top five had evaded being one of Barnes' scalps. But he was already - as the later Tests were to emphasise - Barnes' rabbit!

Sydney Barnes' final figures for that innings were 23 overs, nine maidens, five wickets for 44 runs. Jack Fingleton, the illustrious Australian batsman of the Bradman era and a great cricket pundit, described the scene thus:

Spectators cheered Barnes all the way to the pavilion when the innings ended. It was said of Barnes then that he was too reserved, too stern, to be popular with his fellows, but I imagine that he, like the latter-day O'Reilly, looked upon all batsmen as his natural enemies. Not for him frivolities on the field or the happy exchange of pleasantries. He meant business from the first ball, and never more than on that Melbourne morning of December 30, 1911.

Whereas the more gentlemanly-inclined English crowds found his behaviour a little boorish, in Australia he was a great hero. Of all cricket-playing nations Australia have always admired a fierce competitor. Only in Australia did Barnes receive the acclaim his performances richly deserved. It was his ninth haul of five wickets or more in an innings in only his fourteenth Test, and the sixth time he had performed the feat in Australia.

Wilfred Rhodes flourished in his new role. His sixty-one, along with a century from the Middlesex all-rounder J.W.Hearne, gave England a useful 81-run lead. The wicket had eased by the time Australia batted again. Barnes and Foster, however, once again bowled superbly. Barnes played the junior partner this time, taking three for 96, whilst Foster took the glory with six for 91. Armstrong, with 90, was the mainstay of Australia's 299. For the record, two of Barnes' victims in this innings were the great Victor Trumper, for two, and the skipper Clem Hill for a duck. Hobbs and Rhodes set about the 219 target with skill and enthusiasm, taking the score to 57 before Tibby Cotter had Rhodes caught by Carter for twenty-eight. Hobbs carried on plundering the Australian attack, completing the first of his twelve Test centuries against Australia, as England strolled past their target for the loss of just two wickets. Sydney Barnes now had twenty-eight of his 79 Test wickets at the Melbourne Cricket Ground.

As Australia crumbled, England prospered. In Adelaide Barnes, with three for 77, and Foster, with a marvellous five for 36, dismissed Australia on the first day for 133. Hobbs, with his highest ever Test score, 187, supported by Foster (71) and Rhodes (59), gave England an unassailable 368-run lead. Hill (98), Carter (72), Bardsley (63) and Matthews (53) attempted to retrieve the situation before Barnes, with five for 105, ended their brave effort. Left with 109 to win it was Rhodes who now put the Australian bowlers to the sword with 57 not out as England went two-one up in the series.

England regained the Ashes for the first time since 1905 in a truly remarkable game at Melbourne with one of the greatest performances by an England team in Ashes history. Barnes, with five for 74, and Foster, with four for 77, were again the main destroyers as Australia were shot out for 191. Not only did England then pile up what was the highest Test score up to that date, 589, which was not beaten until another famous England team scored 636 in the second Test at Sydney on the 1928/29 tour, but Hobbs (178), with a record third consecutive Test century, and Rhodes (179), with his highest Test score, produced a world record 323-run opening partnership. Foster weighed in with his third half century of the tour and Woolley scored the first half century of his long and illustrious Test career for good measure. After that performance Australia were finished. Douglas picked up five for 46, Foster three for 38 and Barnes two for 47 as Australia capitulated for 173, giving England victory by the huge margin of an innings and 225 runs.

To rub salt into the wounds of an appallingly subjugated Australia, England crowned the Ashes triumph with their fourth victory in the final Test in Sydney by seventy runs. Frank Woolley's majestic undefeated 133 enabled England to score 324. Barnes was again the leading performer with the ball as he grabbed three for 56 - including the wicket of Trumper for five - whilst the rest of the wickets were shared in Australia's first innings of 176. England then hurried to 214 all out, thanks to Hobbs' and Rhodes' 76-run opening stand. The coup-de-grace was supplied by Foster (4 for 43) and Barnes (4 for 106).

The dismissal of Warwick Armstrong in the second innings was Barnes' hundredth Test wicket, a figure achieved in only seventeen Tests, equalling the record of Australia's Charlie Turner. But Turner played at a time when pitches were not as good - and international batsmen not so refined - whilst Sydney Barnes straddled the Golden Age of batsmanship. His hundred wickets in just seventeen Tests still stands today as a record. The series had been won by four Tests to one. It was the first time England had won four Tests on an Australian tour, a record that has been equalled, in 1928/9 and 1932/3, but never bettered.

There is no doubt that this England team had developed into a fine side. In the debate on whether this was the best ever England team Pelham Warner says:

The England XI of 1902 certainly bristled with illustrious names - Ranji, Fry, MacLaren, Jackson, Jessop, Hirst, Rhodes, Lockwood, Braund, Lilley and J T Tyldesley - and there are those who contend that no English side since then could look at it. While in no way lacking in admiration for this great side, I hold the view that the M.C.C. Australian teams of 1911/12, 1928/29 and 1932/33 would, were such a match possible, make them gallop all the way, and possibly defeat them.

That this touring team are not universally viewed as the greatest ever England team is due to its success being down to key personnel rather than the team as a whole. Warner rationalises it thus: *"The 1911/12 team possessed not only an outstanding pair of batsmen in Hobbs and Rhodes, but an incomparable pair of bowlers in Barnes and Foster. Australian opinion is almost unanimous that they were the best pair of bowlers England has ever sent to Australia".*

By taking thirty-four wickets in the series Sydney Barnes had created a new England Ashes record, beating Tom Richardson's thirty-two wickets on the 1894/5 tour, and, at the same time, equalling George Giffen's Australian record from that same series. It was a remarkable feat that he was very soon to eclipse. Of course, he received support which he would have loved to have had in his previous Test matches. Frank Foster claimed thirty-two wickets and finished top of the averages, whilst Douglas (15) and Woolley (8) were the finest of understudies. The distinguished cricket historian A.A.Thomson says, *"Barnes and Foster did not so much* *defeat the enemy as bowl them out of existence. "*On the batting side, Jack Hobbs produced a record aggregate of 662 runs at an average of 82.75 and Wilfred Rhodes totalled 463 at 57.87. They were supplemented by Woolley's 289 at 48.16 and by Foster, who proved what a tremendous all-round cricketer he was by adding 226 runs to his wickets. Douglas, after his gaffe in the first Test, eventually established himself as a worthy captain. If the tourists were overjoyed, the English cricket public were jubilant. *"There is no doubt that the success of the tour helped to rehabilitate confidence in English cricket which was thought to be on the downward grade"*, remarked Sydney Smith.

Sydney Barnes now had 101 Test wickets at an average of 21.44. He had become only the second Englishman to pass the hundred-wicket milestone. Although he was never to tour Australia again, he had made a lasting impression on that country's cricketing psyche. Feared and admired, he had become the most successful bowler ever to perform under Australian conditions. His total of 77 wickets in only thirteen Tests was, up to that time, the highest number of wickets taken by an individual bowler in Australia in Ashes Test history.

10.

TRIANGULAR TRIUMPH

What was loudly trumpeted as the future of Test cricket - and its World Championship - took place in England in the Summer of 1912. The idea had been conceived in the latter years of the previous decade when the South African team at last became capable of competing on equal terms with both England and Australia. The South African's trouncing of M.C.C.'s 1905/6 tourists and their narrow defeat in England in 1907 made the prospect of such a contest enticing to the cricket administrators of England. Thus, the groundwork was laid for what promised to be a competitive series of nine Tests.

It was expected to be a commercial as well as a cricketing success. In fact, the only worry was that the England side would be the makeweights of the trio, as shown by one spectator's sarcastic comment during the Oval Test of 1909: *"If we don't buck up, we'll have to content ourselves with providing the umpires when Australia and South Africa are here in 1912!"* The reality was very different. The only winners from the Triangular Tournament of 1912 were England, who went through the series of games undefeated by winning four and drawing two, and Sydney Barnes, who added even more records to his already burgeoning position in Wisden's annual almanack.

The reasons for the unmitigated disaster of the Triangular Tournament were many and varied. Firstly, one thing that no one could make allowances for was the weather.

The summer of 1912 made 1902 and 1903 look like drought-afflicted years. Rain decimated not only the County Championship, but also caused the abandonment of three of the nine Tests. The administrators were lucky that six of the Tests reached a conclusion. Secondly - and more importantly - the organisers over-estimated the public's desire to see Australia and South Africa play each other in England. Moreover, in an age of rising unemployment, many felt unable to afford to watch England play both Australia and South Africa in a single season. Thus, the tournament was a financial disaster and was one reason why the experiment was not repeated for many years, and why, some sixty-three years later, administrators were worried about the viability of the first World Cup.

Despite these factors the tournament could still have been a success but for the weaknesses in the teams sent by the South African and Australian authorities. South Africa had declined appreciably since their outstanding performances in the middle of the previous decade. The googly bowlers, Schwarz, Vogler and White, were no longer as effective as they had been previously and struggled on the hard, flat wickets of Australia on their tour of 1910/11. In any case, it was doubtful whether they would have thrived as much as in 1907 because of the abundance of this type of bowler now operating in the county game. Faulkner and Pegler were forced to carry the attack, whilst A.D.Nourse and Herbie Taylor were the only batsmen of Test class - and even this pair had trouble against the exquisite bowling of Sydney Barnes.

The biggest disappointment, however, was the Australian team. Chris Harte, in his epic 'A History of Australian Cricket,' describes the Australian squad as *"the weakest and worst behaved"* to have ever visited England. Apparently they *"set all records for alcohol consumption, disorderly conduct and fraternising with the locals"*. So much so, in fact, that they were eventually *"socially ostracised by their hosts."* This is, indeed, a damning indictment of these Australian tourists and perhaps unprecedented in the history of any country's involvement in Test cricket.

The reason for the fallibility of the Australian team was the absence of Clem Hill, Victor Trumper, Warwick Armstrong, Herbie Carter, Vernon Ransford and Tibby Cotter, their six leading players. Whereas the administrators in England had long since gained control of the game, in Australia it was a protracted and bloody war which they had appeared to win by 1907. The blood-letting, however, continued, reaching a nadir in player/administrator relationships whilst England and Sydney Barnes were romping to their biggest ever victory on Australian soil in 1911/12. Chris Harte sums up what happened in these terms:

The players of those early years had controlled the game...they bitterly opposed handing over the administration of the game to men who had never played top-class cricket. In the forthcoming clashes lifelong friendships were to be broken and only the intervening European war calmed matters down.

The Australian Cricket Board had taken control of Australian cricket gradually during the previous decade and the 1912 tour was the first under their total jurisdiction. Previously the players had chosen a tour manager and wanted Frank Laver, who had done such an excellent job in 1905 and 1909. The Board wanted their own appointee but, apparently, had agreed to let the players choose. Furthermore, Australian players had always done well financially out of tours to England. Syd Gregory, who captained the 1912 team on his eighth trip, made a profit of between four hundred and eight hundred pounds every time with the exception of 1893. The tour manager also received an equal share. The Board not only wanted to impose their own manager, but also have his expenses met out of the total profit rather than his personal share. In 1909 they had also tried to make the players accept a lump sum of four hundred pounds, but the players had successfully negotiated that deal out of their contracts and been rewarded with an extra seventy-three pounds. Because of the failure of the Triangular Tournament, the four tourists who had judiciously accepted the lump sum offer this time came off best whilst the rest had to share a loss.

Matters came to a head between the Board and the *"Big Six"* when, with Australia suffering calamitous reverses on the field, Clem Hill was involved in the unedifying spectacle of a fist fight with Peter McAlister, a friend of the Board and their first choice as tour manager. In the end G.S.Crouch was appointed as manager, but he was an unmitigated disaster, as evidenced by the Australians' behaviour in England. One can only guess at Sydney Barnes' reaction to the disarray in the Australian camp. It is possible that he was envious of the player power which the Australians exhibited at this time and wished that more of his fellow professionals had shown the same degree of obstinacy as he had done in the early years of the century. But, unquestionably, he was the man who exploited their weaknesses to the full.

Plum Warner describes the situation thus: *"At the present time Australian cricket is honeycombed with an amount of personal feeling and bitterness that is incredible and this must, to some extent, have militated against our opponents showing their true form."* Monty Noble, who had by now retired from Test cricket but had prevented a rebellion in 1909 with some skilled diplomacy, lays the blame fairly and squarely at the door of the Australian Cricket Board with this condemnatory statement:

I am a strong supporter of the Board as a Board, and I believe in the principle of Board control, but I am strongly against its present personnel...In these six years they have not been credited with one single act of conciliation and forbearance. They have held the pistol of coercion at the heads of the players the whole time, and gradually taken from them all their privileges.

As a result a weakened Australian team, led by the forty-two year old Syd Gregory, whom many experts felt should not have toured in 1909 because of his age, arrived in England for the summer's cricket.

Meanwhile, Sydney Barnes warmed up for the forthcoming series of Tests with four for 27 and three for 59 and four for 38 and two for 65 in the M.C.C. Australian XI's two innings victories over The Rest at the Oval and Lord's in May. The first game produced another hat-trick to follow the one he claimed for the Players against the Gentlemen at Lord's in 1909. He was now firmly established as English cricket's bowling spearhead, and, with Frank Foster taking three for 71 and three for 67 in the second game, this great pairing showed that they intended to carry on where they had left off in Australia.

The first game of the Triangular Tournament took place at Old Trafford on the 27th and 28th May between Australia and South Africa. Only a small crowd turned up to see Australia destroy the weak South African team by an innings and 88 runs. Charlie Kelleway, with 114, and Warren Bardsley, with 121, were the top scorers in the Australians' total of 448. South Africa did well in their first innings - scoring 265 - but subsided to 95 all out in the follow on, with Kelleway completing an excellent all-round game by taking five for 33. The game was most notable for the amazing performance of Australia's Jimmy Matthews, who claimed a hat-trick in each innings, a feat which has never been repeated.

On the 10th, 11th and 12th June England made their first appearance of the tournament at Lord's against South

Africa. Once again South Africa were beaten by an innings. Reggie Spooner scored 119 in England's total of 337, whilst Sydney Barnes began his record-breaking Summer. Supported by Frank Foster (five for 16), Barnes took five for 25 in South Africa's miserly total of 58. With six for 85 in South Africa's second innings 217, Barnes completed his twelfth and thirteenth instances of five wickets or more in a Test innings and his second ten-wicket haul in a match. He also began a sequence of seven Tests against South Africa in which he was to take five wickets in an innings on no less than twelve occasions, and ten wickets in a match in an unprecedented six of those seven Tests.

Remaining at Lord's for the third game, England took on Australia in an eagerly-awaited clash on the 24th, 25th and 26th June. Rain ruined the game, however. England declared on 310 for seven, with Jack Hobbs scoring another century, whilst the Australians managed 282 - also for seven - when the game was abandoned. Amazingly, Barnes failed to take a single wicket in this innings, conceding 74 runs in thirty-one overs. Charlie Macartney, one of the few batsmen to dominate Barnes for long periods in Test cricket, made 99 and Kelleway 61. Kelleway, Bardsley and Macartney, were the only members of this Australian touring side to enhance their reputations during 1912.

A disappointing crowd turned up at Leeds for England's second fixture against South Africa on the 8th, 9th and 10th July. This time it was a much closer game. South Africa bowled their hosts out twice for 242 and 238, Spooner again showing his evident fondness for the South African's bowling with 82 in the second innings. But Sydney Barnes again proved too much for the South African's batting. In the first innings he took six for 52 out of 147 all out, and completed another ten-wicket haul with four for 63 out of 159 all out in the second innings. He now had twenty-one wickets in just two Tests against the South Africans at little over ten runs apiece. Yet his best was still to come.

Kelleway and Bardsley repeated their performances of their first encounter with South Africa in the next game with a century apiece as Australia cantered to another easy victory - this time by ten wickets. It was followed by yet another rain-affected game between England and Australia at Old Trafford. The Australians were on fourteen without loss in reply to England's 203 all out, Wilfred Rhodes hitting no less than 92 of that total, when the game was abandoned - much to the obvious frustration of a Manchester public, who were to grow accustomed to seeing Test matches ruined by the weather. Sydney Barnes was denied another chance to show his former county what they had been missing over the previous decade.

August did not bring any better weather, but South Africa put up a better showing in their final abandoned game of the tournament against Australia. Nourse scored 64 in their highest total of the series, 329, whilst their bowlers then polished off the Australians for 219 before the game came to its damp conclusion. Thanks to Sydney Barnes, however, their improvement was short-lived. With thirteen wickets for only 57 runs Barnes destroyed the South African batting in the eighth Test, in the process creating a record against South Africa which he was subsequently to break himself. In the first innings he took five for 28, but his second innings eight for 29 was, up to this point, his best individual performance in Test cricket. South Africa were beaten by ten wickets and had now lost five of their six games. Wisden's report on this magnificent spell of bowling unequivocally sums up the skill of Sydney Barnes:

Barnes surpassed himself, bowling in even more deadly form than in the previous Test matches. He broke both ways and his length was irreproachable. The South Africans thought they had never faced bowling quite so difficult.

His total of thirty-four victims still stands as the highest number of wickets taken by an England bowler in a series against South Africa in England. His average of just over eight runs per wicket is an unprecedented feat in this standard of cricket. It was a remarkable performance in a three-match series, straining credulity to its limits, especially considering the fact that Frank Foster had met with nothing like the success of his new ball partner. Both England and Australia had now played five Tests and won three and two respectively. England versus Australia at the Oval on the 19th, 20th, 21st and 22nd August was, therefore, to be the deciding Test of the Triangular Tournament and was to crown a magnificent year for England and for Sydney Barnes.

Batting first, England began in the best possible fashion. Hobbs and Rhodes continued their good work at the top of the order, taking the score to 107 before a minor collapse saw England slump to 144 for five. A revival, led by Woolley's 62, saw England to 245 all out. England took the field determined to impose their superiority on this Australian combination. It was Sydney Barnes who led the England attack. Dismissing Syd Gregory for a single, caught by Rhodes, and then bowling Charlie Macartney for four, he had Australia reeling at 19 for two. Kelleway and Bardsley attempted a recovery, adding 71 runs before Barnes, aided by Frank Woolley, swept through the last eight wickets for a mere twenty-one runs. Woolley took five for 29 but Barnes, bowling unchanged throughout the innings, sent down twenty-seven overs, fifteen of which were maidens, and took five wickets for just thirty runs. It was a sensational performance and these were to be his last wickets in Ashes Tests.

England's 134-run lead was extended to 309 in their second innings. Their captain, C.B.Fry, top scored with 79 in the second innings before Woolley, completing an outstanding match with five for 20, and Harry Dean, with four for 19, destroyed any hope the Australians had of getting back in the game. Having been 46 for one, they were demolished for 65. England had won the game by 244 runs and the Triangular Tournament. Barnes' contribution in that second innings was just four overs for eighteen runs. He had bowled his last ball in Tests against Australia.

As if to underline his tremendous form of the Summer, he turned out in mid-September for C.B.Fry's XI in the Australians' final tour match. Even though Fry's team contained seven England players it was expected that the Australians would show that they were not as bad as some experts had commented. But, thanks to Sydney Barnes, they returned to Australia suitably chastened. On the first morning Barnes took six wickets for only 27 runs to help skittle the Australians out for 72. Although they recovered in their second innings it did not stop them falling to a humiliating eight-wicket defeat. Undoubtedly, the Australians were now glad to see the back of Sydney Barnes.

Many observers have pointed to the weaknesses in the Australian and South African sides as the reason why England were so successful in this series. However, defeat may have been possible if the England selectors had been as profligate with their resources as they had been in 1909 and 1902. But in 1912 all the right things were done. To begin with the ideal candidate, C.B.Fry, was appointed captain. He proved to be an inspirational leader. When originally asked to captain the side he had given the M.C.C. an ultimatum: *"I would accept the captaincy only for the whole of the matches and on condition that I myself was one of the Selection Committee of three, the others to be suitable men neither of them a candidate for a place in the eleven. No others co-opted,"* he wrote in his memoirs. The result was consistent selection of the best elevens England could muster and, inevitably, an undefeated season.

The achievements of England's cricketers certainly cheered the country after the disasters involving the Titanic and Captain Scott. As for Barnes, he had enjoyed an unprecedented Test match season by taking thirty-nine wickets in total at just over ten runs apiece. He had now collected 140 Test wickets at 17.93. It was the highest number of wickets for England in Test matches so far and, in the process, he had beaten Bobby Peel's England record of 102 wickets in Ashes Tests. Although he did not know it at the time, he had played his last game against Australia and his record of 106 wickets at 21.58 was to remain a record until beaten by the forty-nine year old Wilfred Rhodes in 1926.

In its review of the 1912 season, Wisden gives pride of place once again to the astonishing performances of Sydney Barnes:

Barnes surpassed himself, giving conclusive evidence that he is, at the present time, the best bowler in the world. One did not know before that he could, against first-rate batsmen, be quite so deadly on sticky wickets. Bowling that looked more difficult from the ring than his on the second day of the South Africans' match at the Oval I have never seen. The skill with which he broke both ways, while keeping a perfect length all the time, was wonderful.

As he approached his fortieth birthday the stage was set for the greatest exhibition of bowling in Test history.

11.

KING OF THE VELD

The final act of Sydney Barnes' remarkable Test career occurred during the Winter of 1913/14. As the people of Europe nervously awaited the outbreak of hostilities - which was later to be termed *"the war to end all wars"* but which quite palpably was not - England's cricketers enjoyed, as Wisden put it, *"uninterrupted success"* on their tour of South Africa. Sydney Barnes' only trip to the southern tip of the African continent began in triumph, peaked with a performance that will never be erased from Test match record books, and ended in acrimony, with a display of petulance of Barnesian proportions.

With no Test series scheduled between the end of the Triangular Tournament and the visit to South Africa it seemed as if Barnes could have contented himself with rolling over opposition teams in league cricket and for Staffordshire in the Minor Counties Championship. However, he warmed up for the South African tour by easily finishing top of the first class rankings at the end of the 1913 season without playing in a single county game. In four top class representative fixtures he was to take no fewer than thirty-five wickets at just over ten runs apiece, putting an indecent distance between himself and the second-placed bowler in the averages.

Quite surprisingly for a man of Barnes' character and outlook, he had become almost a regular feature in the

114

Gentlemen versus Players matches. Although he missed the 1913 game at Lord's, at the Oval in the middle of July he showed that despite his forty years he was still the world's premier bowler. After taking two for 67 off twenty-five overs in the Gentlemen's first innings when the wicket was at its best, he proceeded to carve through a strong amateur line up in the second. In just nineteen overs he bowled the Players to victory with seven wickets for a miserly 38 runs. He did not appear again on the first class scene until September, when his commitments with Staffordshire and in league cricket were completed.

After Barnes' departure, and in spite of their victory in the 1904 competition, Lancashire had been supplanted by Kent as the main challenger to the hegemony of Lord Hawke's Yorkshire in the County Championship. With Colin Blythe a prolific wicket-taker at county level, supported by Arthur Fielder and D.W.Carr, the addition of the all-round talents of Frank Woolley, and the batting of Seymour, Hutchings, Humphreys, Mason and Hardinge, the Kent XI was one of the strongest and entertaining teams ever seen in the County Championship. After finishing as runners-up to Yorkshire in 1908, they proved irresistible in 1909 and 1910, winning thirty-five of their fifty-one games, to begin what seemed to be turning into a total domination of the pre-war championship. In 1911, with the title decided on percentages - as was the case in every season between 1896 and 1928 - they were beaten into second place by a Frank Foster-inspired Warwickshire by a mere 0.16%. And, in 1912, suffering from the prolonged absences of Woolley to the Triangular Tournament, they fell to third behind Yorkshire and Northamptonshire, despite gaining victories in more matches than any other county. With no distractions in 1913 they returned to their former glory, winning twenty of their twenty-eight fixtures and losing just three.

Once again they were champions - and long before the

end of the season as well - enabling popular representative games to be played in September against select elevens consisting mainly of players South Africa-bound for the winter. It was inevitable that Sydney Barnes would find himself in those elevens that competed against the best team that, arguably, the County Championship had ever seen. It seemed as equally predestined that Barnes would show the insular world of county cricket exactly what it had been missing over the previous decade.

He began by returning seven for 88 for Lionel Robinson's XI against J.R.Mason's Kent XI at the beginning of the month at Old Buckenham Hall in Attleborough. Barnes' old mentor, Archie MacLaren, was now Robinson's secretary and played a major role in attracting top class cricket to the Attleborough ground. At Scarborough a few days later he produced figures of two for 40 and six for 39 for Lord Londesborough's XI against the full Kent county side. By the middle of the month, and having seen off Kent in no uncertain fashion, he played for The Rest of England against a combined Kent and Yorkshire XI at the Oval, in what amounted to a full-scale warm-up game for the forthcoming tour. After beginning in gentle style, with four for 59 off thirty-two overs in the first innings of the strong combined team, he gave notice of what South Africa could expect over the next six months. In the second innings, off just 16.2 overs, ten of which were maidens, he bowled The Rest to victory with seven wickets for only 20 runs. It was another astonishing performance from Sydney Barnes at a ground which had become one his favourites following the nine wickets for the Players against the Gentlemen, his thirteen for 57 against South Africa in 1912, and his five for 30 in the first innings of his last Test against Australia, which had been so instrumental in the Triangular Tournament triumph.

Thus, Barnes was in the form of his life when England left for the Cape in the autumn. In his last ten first class games

- all against top class opposition - he had taken seventy-four wickets for only 633 runs. It is a performance that has few parallels in the history of cricket. Perhaps, then, there is little surprise about what he was about to achieve in South Africa, especially as Wisden, summing up the tour in its 1915 edition, describes England's opposition as *"having struck a very lean period"*, and that they *"were far below their standard of a few years back"*. The South African team of the middle years of the first decade of the 20th Century had broken up just when it looked like they were about to make a breakthrough into the previously nepotic world of Test cricket. Disappointing in 1912 - despite a late rally - they had been further weakened *"by a strange irony of fate"*, as Wisden terms it, when Schwarz, Vogler and Faulkner of the fine 1907 side, and Pegler - who had carried their bowling attack so well during the Triangular Tournament - decided to remain in England after 1912.

But this quartet were all primarily bowlers and none of South Africa's major batsmen, with the exception of Charlie Llewellyn, were unavailable. Moreover, in Herbie Taylor, a young player who had created such a good impression in 1912, they had a batsman who was developing into one of the world's outstanding stroke-makers. In fact, in 1913/14 he was to average over fifty in the five-Test series as well as scoring 91 and 100 for Natal in the tourists' only defeat of the campaign. Taylor became one of the few batsmen ever to master Sydney Barnes, much to the latter's frustration, as was soon to become evident. Whereas Barnes was to scythe through almost every team he appeared against, the contest between these two great cricketers was to be amongst one of the most gripping in Test match history, bringing out the best in Taylor and - unfortunately - the worst in Sydney Barnes.

Talking some years later, H.G.Owen-Smith, an outstanding all-rounder in the 1929 South African touring side, says this of Taylor and his great battle with Barnes in 1913/14: *"He made S F Barnes look like an ordinary bowler. Barnes was bowling, and Herbie used to move his right leg across behind the off-stump and touch him round the corner for four. It got to the stage when Barnes actually threw the ball on the ground and said he wasn't going to bowl any more."* It seems truly remarkable, therefore, that this typical display of petulance came amid Barnes' most prolific feat. One can see his burning desire to master all batsmen in Owen-Smith's comments and, paradoxically, the tantrums that would ensue if a batsman had the temerity to challenge his technique with skill and speed of thought every bit the equal of that he displayed.

Even his most ardent admirers could not have predicted that during the whole tour he would claim 125 victims in only fourteen matches, at an average of 9.64. Of those 125 wickets, 104 were in official first class games. Only one other bowler has taken more than 100 wickets in a South African season. During 1957/58 Richie Benaud was to break Barnes' record with 106 victims. But Benaud's record was created in eighteen games, as opposed to Barnes' twelve, and at an average of 19.39 compared to Barnes' 10.74. Nor could they have dreamt that in only four of the five Tests he would take a world record forty-nine dismissals at an average of 10.93. It is a series record which has only ever remotely been threatened once, by Jim Laker on the helpfully wet wickets of the English Summer of 1956. And most experts were to be astonished that in a single Test match an individual bowler could take seventeen of the twenty wickets to fall as he did at Johannesburg in the second Test, thus creating a record that has been surpassed only once - and that by Laker at a damp Old Trafford in that same 1956 series. In short, from a forty year-old medium/fast bowler it was a performance the like of which Test cricket may never experience again.

He began the tour quietly enough, against a South West Districts XV in the middle of November. Touring sides at this time still played representative games against teams of more than eleven players, usually to make the games more competitive and to give a chance to as many promising locals as possible. In the first innings he took just a single wicket for 28 runs, before demolishing the home side second time around with seven for 11 off ten overs. Then, in the first provincial match of the tour, he took two for 34 and a brilliant seven for 25 against Cape Province. Against a Grahamstown and Colleges XV a few days later he had the astonishing match figures of thirteen for 48 in 26.5 overs, before warming up for the first Test with four for 36 and two for 21 against The Border XI.

He had already taken a remarkable thirty-six wickets in four games at less than six runs apiece when the first Test at Durban began on December 13th, 1913. It was to signal the start of Barnes' record-breaking winter - and also his duel with Herbie Taylor. South Africa were shot out on the first day for 182, with Barnes being easily the most successful bowler, taking five for 57. But Taylor almost carried his bat through the innings, being last man out after scoring a brilliant 109, having played Barnes *"with perfect confidence"* as Wisden reports. Thanks to a century from Johnnie Douglas and 82 from Jack Hobbs, England piled up a total of 450. Barnes then trapped Taylor leg before for eight in the South African second innings, before finishing with five for 48 from twenty-five overs. Only Nourse, with 46, showed much resistance as England swept to victory by an innings and 157 runs.

There was just one tour match - against Transvaal - before the second and third Tests, both at Johannesburg. Evidently Barnes took things easy in this game. His four for 78 in the first innings completed his fifty wickets for the tour, whilst second time around he bowled just thirteen overs, taking three for 31. It was during the last few days of 1913, at that second Test in Johannesburg, that Barnes was to produce his individual Test bowling record. At the same time that his finest hour had arrived pandemonium was breaking out all around Johannesburg. Gold and diamond miners, as well as railwaymen, were initiating a general strike. History is littered with instances where great deeds take place in circumstances where attention is drawn elsewhere. Let us not forget the cataclysm which was about to engulf Europe as well. As industrial strife gripped Johannesburg Sydney Barnes, spurred on no doubt by the assertive South African working man, produced his finest exhibition. Wisden describes the game thus:

It was Barnes's match. On no occasion was the great bowler seen to quite such advantage. He took seventeen wickets - 8 for 56 and 9 for 103 - proving quite irresistible on the last morning.

It was a performance that still stands in second place on the all-time Test bowling lists. None of the other England bowlers, who included Woolley, Douglas and Rhodes, were anywhere near as effective. Ironically, the South Africans batted better in this game. Taylor made 29 and 40, while Nourse made a second innings 56, but England still won by an innings after Wilfred Rhodes (152) and Philip Mead (102) had enabled England to score over 400 again.

The third Test, which began on New Year's Day 1914, was a much closer affair and the only occasion in seven consecutive Tests against South Africa that Barnes did not take ten wickets or more in the match. Jack Hobbs hit 92 on the first day, but England could manage only 236 all out. The South Africans, however, also struggled, limping to 151. Hearne, with five for 49, was the main recipient of their batsmen's generosity, whilst Barnes took just three wickets for 26 in sixteen overs. Thanks to Mead (86) and Douglas (77) England left South Africa a target of 396 to win. It was here that Barnes began to become frustrated with the ease with which Taylor was making his bowling look nondescript. As Taylor, with 70, and Zulch, with 83, added 153 for the first wicket, and it looked like ending in an improbable victory for the hosts, Barnes enjoyed his worst moments of the tour and his bowling became littered with the inconsistencies with which his detractors in the county game had accused him of ten years earlier. However, after the breakthrough was made he ran through the middle order to finish with five for 102 and give England victory by 91 runs. In three Tests he had an aggregate of thirty-five wickets, already equalling George Lohmann's series record against South Africa with two Tests still to play.

In between the third match of the series and his final appearance in Test cricket he continued to decimate all opposition. Against Griqualand West he took five for 22 in both innings and, with seven for 41 and six for 38, he completed 100 wickets for the tour against the Orange Free State. It had come in only ten games, a truly remarkable performance. Many commentators suggest that he now relaxed, having decided that the competition was too easy, but the final confrontation with Herbie Taylor was still to come. Against Transvaal he had his most ineffective game of the whole tour, with three for 94 and nought for 25, and then, even though he took five for 44 in the first innings, he was comprehensively taken apart by Taylor in the second innings of the return fixture with Natal. He took just two wickets for 70 runs in seventeen overs as a Taylor century, following a first innings 91 out of 153, saw Natal to 216 for five and England's only defeat of the entire tour. It was here that Sydney Barnes finally cracked at the antics of Herbie Taylor in daring to treat him like some second-rate medium-pacer. As Natal edged towards victory Taylor farmed the strike, playing Barnes with ease and scoring most of his runs off the master bowler. At the end of an over where the South African upstart had once again stole a single to take the strike, Barnes is reported to have whined: *"It's Taylor, Taylor, Taylor. All the time!"*

A buoyant South Africa began the fourth Test at Durban in good heart, despite the fact a series victory was now beyond them. Not only was it to prove to be South Africa's best performance of the series, but Barnes was also to respond with his second best Test match return. In 29.5 overs he was instrumental in dismissing the South Africans for 170 first time round, taking seven for 56. England's batting failed, however. Only Jack Hobbs, with 64, could cope with Carter, Blanckenberg and Newberry as - for the first time - South Africa gained a first innings advantage. 93 by Taylor, and some good scoring down the order, extended the advantage to 312. The acrimonious duel between the master bowler and the intelligent South African batsman was won by the latter, but Barnes still picked up another seven wickets for 88 in the second innings of this, his twenty-seventh and final Test match. Astonishingly, his last 100 Test wickets had taken just twelve matches, a feat that has never been remotely threatened. Hobbs again shouldered England's batting, with 97, but England were hanging on at 154 for five when the game finally ended as a draw.

As well as being his last Test, Barnes was to appear in no further tour games. His England career had ended on a high, even though, as we shall see later in the Barnes story, he could very easily have played again and he was about to prove that he was every bit as cantankerous at forty as he had been at thirty. Arriving in Bloemfontein in preparation for the fifth Test he was unhappy at the South African's failure to carry out their promise of special reward for his performances. So upset was he that he refused to play again on the tour. It was a disturbing - but entirely characteristic - end to the England career of Sydney Francis Barnes.

Over the years many so-called experts have attempted to devalue the achievements of Barnes in South Africa during the 1913/14 tour. They have pointed to the matting wickets and weaknesses in the opposition as reasons for seeing his records as practically worthless. But, undoubtedly, there have been weaker Test teams than the 1913/14 South Africans. The batting of Taylor and, to a lesser extent, Nourse, Zulch and Hands, was of Test class. More potent opportunities for his records to be broken have presented themselves since - as Jim Laker was to prove over forty years later - especially with the amount of Test cricket played nowadays. The reality is that it was a scarcely believable display of skill and endeavour. His tour record of 125 victims from fourteen games, a fully 68 more than Rhodes' next best of 57, was staggering in the extreme. But forty-nine Test wickets, when the great Wilfred Rhodes took only six, Woolley managed just seven, and Douglas and Relf ten apiece, gives, by way of comparison, an insight into the magnificence of the exploit. No doubt if he had appeared in that final Test, which England incidentally won comfortably, the record he would have created may have been impossible to beat in the future history of the game.

Having treated Barnes with disdain a decade earlier, Wisden now fails to contain its adulation. In its tour summary in the 1915 edition it says of Barnes:

It would be hard indeed to praise him beyond his deserts. Everyone felt sure before he left England, with his remarkable finger spin, he would do well on matting wickets, but his success exceeded all expectation. He was simply irresistible...Moreover, according to common report, he beat the bat about twice an over without hitting the wicket.

He was the most celebrated cricketer in the world. *"Always keeping a good shape and by far less hard to the hands than other makers,"* he is quoted as saying on a full page advertisement in the Wisdens of 1914 and beyond as he extols the virtues of the cricket bible's own brand of "Special Crown" balls. It is a piece of marketing which would fit easily into the crassly commercial world of the late 20th Century, and undoubtedly signifies Barnes' advanced business acumen as well as his unequivocal acceptance by the status quo.

Although approaching his forty-first birthday, Sydney Barnes still had more Test victims ahead of him. 189 Test wickets was an extraordinary aggregate which would take nearly thirty years for any other bowler to overhaul. Furthermore, he had done this in only twenty-seven Tests, and at the remarkably low average of 16.43. All the evidence pointed to his improvement with age and more wonderful deeds at Melbourne, the Oval, Sydney, Johannesburg and Lord's to come.

But storm clouds were gathering over Europe. Within a few months of the tourists' return to England Archduke Franz Ferdinand, the heir to the Austro-Hungarian Empire, was assassinated in Sarajevo. A chain of alliances - which were thought to guarantee security and prevent confrontation - activated themselves. By the beginning of August war had broken out. With respect to the ensuing conflict first class cricket ground to a halt by mid-August, not to return until 1919 when English cricket discovered the extent of the tragedy.

12.

BARNES AND THE LEAGUES

With the increasingly serious hostilities in Europe it was felt that competitive sport was too frivolous an occupation and should be abandoned immediately. Of course, there was widespread support for this policy, especially as the prevailing mood seemed to be that the war would be over by Christmas. The conflict, however, lasted for four long years. Nearly three quarters of a million Englishmen were to lose their lives, amongst them many hundreds of cricketers.

Even though the County Championship remained dormant between 1914 and 1918, league cricket became a focal point for passionate cricket devotees. One league which was to flourish above all others during the war was the Bradford League. Sydney Barnes was, at forty-one, considered too old for the immediate influx of volunteers that marched merrily to their deaths or incapacitation on the Western Front, despite being fit and active enough to be considered the best bowler in the world. He became one of the Bradford League's premier recruits, playing for Saltaire from 1915 until 1923, but was by no means its only famous conscript. Cec Parkin, who was to gain so much inspiration from Barnes over the next decade or so, turned out for Undercliffe whilst working as a fuel overseer in Oswald-twistle. He was joined by Charlie Llewellyn, one of the more successful members of the South African team from the Triangular Tournament, and the Nottinghamshire and

England batsman George Gunn.

Apart from Barnes the most famous cricketer to ply his trade in the Bradford League during the war was Jack Hobbs. Young men who avoided active service during the Great War were often shunned by society, but this does not appear to have happened to the great Jack Hobbs. In his autobiography, 'My Cricket Memories', Hobbs explains his absence from the carnage of Le Cateux, the Marne and the Somme by saying his financial position *"left room for improvement"*. He had a wife, four young children and a widowed mother and, even though he was now the best batsman in England, his employers at Surrey County Cricket Club never saw fit to reward him with a wage which fully represented his status. As a character Jack Hobbs was as far removed from that of Sydney Barnes as anyone was ever likely to be. Not for Hobbs the gruelling and acrimonious negotiations of the proud working man; only deference and a quiet doff of the cap. Hobbs worked in a munitions factory in London for the first two years of the war, commuting to Bradford on Saturdays to play cricket, before the morality of his position became too much for this self-effacing individual and he joined the fledgling Royal Flying Corps.

At one time or another more England cricketers played in the Bradford League. Frank Woolley, Schofield Haigh, Ernest Tyldesley, Jack Hearne, Tom Wass and Bill Hitch all appeared in various teams. Pudsey St Lawrence, that famous breeding ground for future Yorkshire and England players, provided the cricketing interest for the great Herbert Sutcliffe. The war delayed his Yorkshire debut until 1919, and the records of Pudsey St Lawrence do not show his name during this period even though he was a regular member of the team. The reason was that Sutcliffe played under an assumed name because to play for Pudsey he had to absent himself from his barracks at York, where he was a corporal in the Sherwood Foresters, before eventually being promoted to Second

Lieutenant and transferring to the Green Howards in Salisbury.

Sydney Barnes had no need of subterfuge, and it is certain he would have scoffed at the idea of a pseudonym. His magnificent performances in Test cricket over the two years prior to the First World War had made him the most celebrated bowler in cricket history. But to Barnes the absence of county cricket made not a jot of difference to his life as a professional cricketer. For it was in league cricket that he had originally made his name. As the first of many great international stars to make their living in the Lancashire League, he was the man who was to elevate that particular competition to the status of the best known league in the world.

That a conglomeration of small towns in the Lancashire hinterland beyond Manchester became a mecca for most of the world's greatest cricketers is one of the miracles of geography that perhaps only cricket could precipitate. The names of places like Rawtenstall, Ramsbottom, Haslingden, Bacup, Burnley, Lowerhouse, Church, Todmorden, Nelson, Accrington, Enfield, Rishton, and Colne conjure up a picture of cloth caps, whippets and back-to-back terraces. They were the cradle of the Industrial Revolution; mill towns of character and identity; proud communities bonded by common purpose in work and leisure. As the factory system gripped these towns in the 19th Century so cricket developed, not only as pure recreation in itself, but also as a form of inter-town rivalry. Somewhat fierce on occasions, as evidenced by a report in the 'Bacup Times' in the 1870's of *"deplorable ill-spirit and ungovernable excitement"* by spectators during Bacup/Haslingden games; but a rivalry which generated large crowds and an enthusiasm which was to lure some of the world's great talents to this exclusive - but friendly - area of the cricket world.

Even when the competition between these clubs was

disorganised crowds of five or six thousand were not unusual. After a long week in the local factories the workforce were in need of relaxation. The league formed itself around the life of the factories and the needs of the working classes, especially when Saturday became a half day, whilst down the road in Manchester the county game was played during the week to suit the needs of the gentleman amateurs, who often had bigger game to pursue at weekends. Instead of supporting their county, the workers in the mills of Lancashire gave their allegiance to their local clubs. With little travelling required and admission prices low, as well as excellent competitive cricket, it was no surprise to see the grounds of the Lancashire clubs full on a Saturday afternoon, whilst the county ground remained half-empty during the week. As one old mill worker once put it: *"Tha's got to be a man o'means to watch first-class cricket...and besides tha's expected to wear a collar and tie when tha goes to Old Trafford."*

In 1890 representatives of thirteen clubs met at the Commercial Hotel in Accrington and decided that an organised league for clubs in North East Lancashire be formed. The competition proper began in the Summer of 1892, adopting the title of the Lancashire Cricket League. In fact, the 1890's saw the birth of many of the great northern cricket leagues. The Central Lancashire League, in which Barnes also played, was formed in the same year. When the promising bowler Sydney Barnes joined Rishton as groundsman/professional in 1895, the Lancashire League was already established as a major forum for future county performers, county players past their best, and as a conduit for players from other counties hoping to qualify for the more affluent Lancashire county club by means of residence.

The first great signing by the Lancashire League was that of Yorkishire and England bowler Bobby Peel. He moved to Accrington after being unceremoniously sacked by Lord Hawke for persistent drunkenness. Several Nottinghamshire players appeared for various clubs in the Lancashire League having failed to make the grade at their home county, one of the strongest in England at the time. The first was Henry Reynolds, who was engaged by the prosperous Burnley club from 1880 to 1893, having played for Nottinghamshire between 1872 and 1875. Between 1893 and 1897 a number of Nottinghamshire professionals turned out for Lancashire League clubs: Richard Hardstaff at Rawtenstall, William Wilkinson at Todmorden, Frank Shacklock and Arthur Wilkinson at Nelson, Silas Hardy and Ben Gregory at Lowerhouse, Thomas Flowers at Church and Robert Mee at Accrington. All had fairly short county careers except for Shacklock, who appeared 118 times for his home county between 1885 and 1893. In fact, Shacklock was an interesting character. He joined Nelson after being suspended by his county for ill-discipline in August 1893. At the end of his one and only season with Nelson he emigrated to New Zealand to avoid prosecution for debts and re-surfaced in Christchurch thirty years later as an administrator with the Canterbury Cricket Association.

It is hardly surprising - considering his personality - that Sydney Barnes thrived in this atmosphere. He was a champion of the working man, never afraid to air his views and, amongst the more amenable administrators of the Lancashire League, who were constantly hoping to attract more and more quality cricketers from the county game, he was more likely to get his own way when it came to wages and conditions. After five meteorically successful seasons with Rishton, in which he took 411 wickets at a little over nine runs apiece, he moved to Burnley. Burnley was - and still is - one of the biggest towns in this area of Lancashire and therefore hosted an affluent cricket club. Its football club has always been an institution in the town. In fact, when Burnley Football Club appeared in the First Division of the Football League in the 1960's and early 1970's, they regularly secured remarkable crowds of 30,000 or more - almost half its population. It was only a matter of time before Sydney Barnes would be persuaded to use his bargaining power, in terms of his unique ability, to raise his wages. Barnes repaid them in the way he knew best, taking over one hundred wickets in 1900 and 1901.

Although the local public preferred the Lancashire League to the county game, county cricket was still seen as the goal to which the best club players should aspire. So when Lancashire asked Rishton for Barnes' services for the game against Sussex and Tom Richardson's Benefit Match at the Oval on August Bank Holiday 1899, the Lancashire League President, Jimmy Sutcliffe, who was also President of Burnley and had been instrumental in securing Barnes' services for his club for the following season, persuaded him to go. This respect for county cricket, however, was not mutual. Richard Holt in his thorough history, 'Sport and The British', comments thus about the Lancashire League: *"These games could attract large crowds and produced some very fine players despite the contempt in which they were held by the grandees of the county game."* Lord Hawke disliked the leagues, whilst the Lancashire hierarchy dismissed them with ambivalence. History was to prove that this was a mistake of gargantuan proportions. For not only did the Lancashire League pillage world cricket of its greatest stars from the early 1920's onwards, but also if the leagues could turn an unsuccessful county bowler like Sydney Barnes into the best bowler in the world, how many other great talents have been ignored solely because their performances were in this supposedly inferior standard of cricket?

If the attitude of the northern counties towards league cricket was one of sneering disrespect, the counties of the south treated leagues with nothing short of outright contempt. Bernard Hollowood defines the relative difference in approach between north and south thus:

Club cricketers south of Birmingham were apt to condemn the league game as yet another manifestation of the boorishness of the north. In the south cricket was supposed to be a game for gentlemen, a game played in a gentlemanly manner by gentry and yokel alike. It was a game to amuse and interest the performers, and spectators were neither expected nor catered for. The northern game, it was believed, was played as a variant of cock-fighting or rabbit-coursing and was riddled with vested pecuniary interests.

Little wonder, therefore, that Sydney Barnes was treated like he was by the game's grandees in his first few years at the top level. Only by the 1960's and 1970's did competitive league structures form in the south of England, by which time the Lancashire League had played host to many generations of the world's finest cricketers.

The relative value to Burnley of Sydney Barnes was seen in the hundred pounds in compensation they asked for - and received - from the Lancashire club at the end of the 1901 season. But, of course, the county game did not suit his personality. He returned to the Lancashire League in 1904, this time with Church, and began his long career, stretching over thirty-one years, as a minor counties cricketer with his native Staffordshire. It is worth noting that his weekly wage with Church was more than double what he had received eight years earlier in an age when the average working man's pay packet had hardly changed. The hiatus in his career after leaving Lancashire is reflected in his performances for Church in 1904. He took a mere sixty-four wickets, a total which was to remain his worst in league cricket until the season of 1933, when he was in his sixtieth year. However, he also scored 666 runs at an average of 31.17 including an innings of 131 not out. He did much better in 1905, his ninety wickets costing a little over nine runs apiece.

Despite the successes of his two seasons with Church,

the parting of the ways between Sydney Barnes and the Lancashire League club was, predictably, resonant of his dealings with cricket administrators. Church had expected, with Barnes in their side, to win the championship. That they did not was no fault of Barnes, who had batted and bowled as well as anyone in the Lancashire League in 1904 and 1905. Church's secretary offered him reduced terms to return in 1906. Barnes' reply was, once again, entirely typical: *"As much more as you like, but not a penny less and you will pay me more if I play for you again"*, was his forthright answer. Church were unable to acquiesce to his demands and Sydney Barnes was available to the highest bidder again.

The success he engendered from a previously disappointing Staffordshire team saw him revert to his home county to play club cricket. It was the Porthill Park club in the unheralded North Staffordshire League which acquired his services for the next nine seasons, coinciding with his greatest feats in Test cricket. From the start of the summer of 1906, until he at last became an England regular in 1909, he produced an astonishing tally of 437 wickets for Porthill Park. In all for the North Staffordshire League club his haul was 893 wickets at barely five runs apiece. Many of Barnes' detractors have pointed to his disloyalty as a particular deficiency, but from 1904 until the outbreak of war he showed his devotion by playing his cricket in his home county despite the fact he could surely have gone elsewhere and named his price. Not only did he reward them with wickets and 5,625 runs at an average of 42.61, but also, in those nine seasons, Porthill Park won the North Staffordshire League championship no less than six times and were runners-up on the other three occasions, having won the title only once in the fifteen years prior to Barnes' arrival.

It is during this period at Porthill Park that some of the best anecdotal evidence of Barnes' prodigious gifts and menacing character have been recorded. Bernard

132

Hollowood's father, Albert, was probably second only to Sydney Barnes in talent and personality in Staffordshire cricket during the pre-war period. In fact, an article in 'Cricket' magazine in 1911 titled, "A Chat About Staffordshire Cricketers and Cricket", is decorated with pictures of Barnes and Albert Hollowood. His son recounts that Barnes was admonished by his Porthill Park captain for bowling two balls short outside the off stump at Hollowood, which the Burslem batsman dispatched to the boundary. *"You can't bowl outside the off-stump at Albert,"* groaned the skipper, *"it's four every time."* The next ball was pitched in the same place but turned sharply to trap Hollowood LBW. *"See what I mean?"* grunted Barnes, *"What do two fours matter? Two fours are eight: Albert usually gets fifty!"* After that experience Albert Hollowood became adept at scoring runs against Porthill Park by avoiding facing the great Barnes. On one famous occasion Barnes attempted to unhinge Albert with sarcasm:

"Why don't you get up to the other end, Albert?"
"I thought I'd let you have a few easy wickets, Syd?"
"Don't tell me you're scared!"
"Not at all, but I'm getting all the runs I want off Harry, thank you."

Despite the triumphs and the relative cordiality of those nine years at Porthill Park, the manner of his departure had more than a hint of the Divine Right of Barnes. Relations between the club and their superstar were such that - unusually for Barnes - he worked without a contract. *"We seemed too pally to want a legal document"*, was Barnes' explanation years later when describing the crisis that the events of 1914 brought to his life. He had been offered a three-year extension to his contract during the 1914 season, but when the war became imminent Barnes asked the club chairman, J.E.Leigh, what would happen if no cricket were played the following year. *"You can take it from me,"* replied Leigh, *"that whatever happens we shall see you right for at least another year."* In March of 1915 Barnes received a letter from Porthill Park to the effect that the verbal contract was not worth the paper it was written on. Although he sought legal advice he found himself in an impossible position, especially as he was not alone amongst club professionals in having his contract cancelled for the duration of the war. After letting the committee know - in no uncertain terms - what he thought of them, he left the club in acrimony, never to return again.

As one glorious chapter closed in the life of Sydney Barnes so - as is often the case with genius - another opened. Whilst perusing the Athletic News one Friday in April of 1915 Barnes saw an advertisement for a left-arm bowler required. *"Will I do?"* he cabled the desperate club, Saltaire in the Bradford League. *"Come tomorrow. Will arrange terms"*, was their reply, and the legend of Sydney Barnes and the Bradford League had begun. On that first Saturday he began the way he was to continue for next nine years. Bowling Old Lane, the best team in the league at the time, were his unfortunate debut victims as he helped himself to eight wickets for a mere eleven runs. Considering the standard of play in the Bradford League, his performances over nine seasons with the Saltaire club were undoubtedly the most remarkable ever in league cricket. Over 900 wickets at just over five runs apiece, against sides containing two or more first class cricketers, was an incredible achievement and unparalleled in the history of league cricket. One interesting result of his appearance for Saltaire was his acceptance of a compromise on the terms and conditions of his employment. *"Not what I would have liked,"* was his rueful admission in later life of the wage Saltaire offered him. *"But then it was that or nothing as no other cricket was being played in England"*, he magnanimously explained.

If the exodus of county professionals to league cricket

was just a trickle before the First World War, then that trickle became a relative torrent in the years up to the Second World War. Most of the ex-first class players who appeared in the Lancashire League before the Great War were failed county players. Only Sydney Barnes and Cec Parkin were successful at the top level of the game. The abundance of talent in the Bradford League during the war, which led to large crowds and a highly competitive atmosphere, gave the administrators of the various Lancashire League clubs food for thought. The season of 1922 saw the acquisition by the Nelson club of a player who was to transform the Lancashire League into the international force for which Sydney Barnes had been the pathfinder. Ted McDonald, the fearsome Australian fast bowler who had terrorised the finest of England's batsmen in the Summer of 1921, became the Lancashire League's first *"sensation"* signing.

During the Winter of 1921/22 the Australian Cricket Board, on hearing of McDonald's proposed move to Nelson, attempted to dissuade him. Lord Hawke, once again showing his astounding grasp of the future of cricket, was said to be *"delighted to note McDonald's sound refusal"* to take up Nelson's offer of a contract. But McDonald did not refuse. For three years he graced the Lancashire League whilst qualifying to play for the county. Whilst at Lancashire he took nearly 1400 wickets, and helped them to four championships in the late 1920's. After McDonald came Learie Constantine. Constantine lit up the Lancashire League and proved to be a pathfinder for a galaxy of international stars to the mill towns of East Lancashire. From Griffith and Hall to Holding and Roberts, from Lindwall to Lillee, Headley to Richards, Mankad to Walcott, Cec Pepper, Bill Alley, Ian Chappell and Alan Border; since McDonald almost all of the world's foremost cricketers have appeared at one time or another in the Lancashire League.

Immediately after the First World War, however, the

authorities became worried about the situation because, before they realised it was overseas stars that the Lancashire League required, they saw the county game at risk. A. W. Pullin, in his 'History of Yorkshire Cricket 1903-23', writes: *"Yorkshire, like other counties, could not regard it as consistent with their position and reputation that any of their players should find league cricket more financially attractive than that of the county game",* whilst Wisden, as early as 1920, warned of a possible problem: *"The menace of the Lancashire and Yorkshire leagues cannot be ignored...leading professionals constantly receive from league clubs offers of better terms."* The gentlemen administrators of the county game had failed to learn the lessons of labour economics which Sydney Barnes had so assiduously attempted to teach them in the early years of the century.

Though the authorities grumbled and obstructed, and failed to see the benefits of the league game for player and spectator alike, they were powerless to stop cricketers earning their living in this competitive environment. Rumours of defections from the county game became rife. Fred Root, the famous Worcestershire professional of the 1920's and 30's, turned down the offer of six hundred pounds for a twenty-week season. Eventually he did sign for a Lancashire League club - but in 1938 when his county career was effectively over. After the "Bodyline" tour of 1932/3 Harold Larwood became a cause celebre and had to strenuously deny being offered the amazing sum of forty pounds a week by Burnley, whilst the Australian Cricket Board were equally worried about the futures of their own players after McDonald, as shown by their upgrading of the great Don Bradman's contract when rumours circulated that he had signed for Accrington for the astonishing sum of one thousand pounds a year plus various performance bonuses.

Sydney Barnes, meanwhile, continued to ply his trade in the leagues well into his sixties. After spells with Castleton

An original drawing of Sydney Barnes by Louis Ollier

Moor and Rochdale in the Central Lancashire League, he returned to the Lancashire League for Rawtenstall in 1931 and played for three more seasons. His last professional league contract was for the season of 1940, when he was sixty-seven years old, making his professional career the longest there has ever been in the history of the game. In nearly half a century of league cricket he amassed 4,069 wickets at the incredible average of 6.03. One can only assume an ironic smile on his face as players from all corners of the globe began to appear on the stage that he had been the first to captivate more than a generation earlier.

13.

WHEN THE WAR WAS OVER

For Europe the First World War was a tragedy; for English cricket it was a disaster. From 1915 until 1919 the obituary pages of Wisden are littered with many hundreds of names of cricketers who gave their lives for their country. From established Test players, to county cricketers on the fringes of national selection, to promising schoolboys; the war held no respect for reputations or potential.

Colin Blythe was the greatest loss, killed at Passchendale. Sending a man like Blythe - whose sensitivity made him sick with nerves before a Test match - to the Western Front merely serves to emphasise the folly that was the Great War. Amongst the potential Test players who gave their lives was Warwickshire's Percy Jeeves, who hinted at greatness just before the outbreak of war but died on the Somme in 1916. He was later immortalised in the novels of P.G.Wodehouse as the archetypal gentleman's gentleman; the last vestige of the master/servant relationship of Edwardian England that was finally laid to rest by the events of 1914 to 1918. And, of course, there was Major Booth, yet another in the great line of Yorkshire all-rounders, who had performed the "double" of 1,000 runs and 100 wickets in 1913, and must have learnt so much from Sydney Barnes on his only tour to South Africa in 1913/14.

Even though it was England that suffered the most, the cricketers of the colonies of Australia and South Africa also grieved their fallen heroes. Tibby Cotter, heir to the fast bowling throne of 'The Demon' Spofforth and Ernest Jones, never really achieved greatness, but as one of the six who boycotted the Australian team for the Triangular Tournament he had the respect of his peers. He died far from any cricket field - at Beersheba in the Negev desert, now part of the state of Israel - in the campaign on the Eastern Front. Two of that great quartet of South African googly bowlers, who so mesmerised the England touring team of 1905/6, fell victim to the hazards of war. Schwarz and White, the former dying of influenza whilst on active service; the latter of wounds in October 1918 after the armistice had been signed, would never weave their magic again.

But these were not the only losses of 1914-18. Barnes' partner in the destruction of the Aussies in 1911/12, Frank Foster, suffered a horribly broken leg in a motorcycle accident and was forced to retire from first class cricket at the tender age of twenty-five. As if to signal the end of the Golden Age, the great W.G.Grace fell victim to the march of time in 1915; or was it sadness brought on by a world engaging in ritualised slaughter when he was part of a gentler, happier era. Also in 1915 A.E.Stoddart, that magnificent dual rugby and cricket international, who had led his country to glorious Ashes success in 1894/5 in Australia, committed suicide amidst financial and marital strife. Surely, of all war deaths, this summed up the horror of the time. But then, just when the cricket world thought there could be no more wretched grief after the death of W.G. and the demise of Stoddart, came terrible news from Australia: Victor Trumper, scion of the Golden Age, had died in a Sydney hospital. He was thirty-seven years old.

Despite the great upheaval caused by the war cricket soon mobilised itself into action immediately the Armistice was signed. Attendances were expected to fall so a championship was proposed for the 1919 season with games over two days rather than three. When some of the more affluent counties realised the financial and playing implications of a two-day tournament they attempted to have the three-day game re-instated. They felt that many games would end in draws and this would not help the counties attract spectators back in the same numbers as before the war, but they were out-voted by those counties who were suffering the greatest financial hardships.

The predictable result of a two-day championship can be seen in the final table of 1919. Of the 124 games played in 1919 no less than fifty-six ended in draws. Yorkshire finished as champions with the lowest percentage, 46.15, since that system had been introduced in 1896. Moreover, the difference between the number of games played by each county was vast. Yorkshire and Lancashire played twenty-six and twenty-four games respectively, whilst Somerset and Northamptonshire managed only twelve. Only four players: Jack Hobbs, Philip Mead, George Gunn and Patsy Hendren, topped 1,000 runs, and only one bowler, Wilfred Rhodes, took more than 100 wickets. It was a stumbling return for the County Championship.

During the 1919 season an Australian Imperial Forces team toured England. In fact, the Australians had wanted a Test series but the M.C.C. had discouraged the idea because it was felt more time was needed to recover. Instead, they had promised to send a touring team to Australia at the end of the 1920 season when county cricket had more or less returned to normal. The tour turned out to be a triumph for Australian cricket, with bumper crowds and a successful team, but a disaster for English cricket. England lost all five Test matches - all by large margins. It was the first whitewash in Test cricket history. When the England team, accompanied by the Australians, returned for another series in the summer of 1921, the abysmal run continued with Australia winning the first three Tests before England finally salvaged two draws.

Two reasons have consistently been advanced for the calamitous form of the England team. Sydney Smith explains the first in his review of the 1920 tour: *"Australia established a record by winning the five games, but it has to be remembered that it was England's first visit after War No.1, during which she suffered so much."* The second reason was the strength of the Australian team. Warwick Armstrong, Charlie Macartney, Warren Bardsley and Charlie Kelleway - youthful before the war - were now in their prime. In Jim Gregory and Ted Mcdonald they had discovered two opening bowlers who were to be every bit as effective as Frank Foster and Sydney Barnes were in 1911/12. Add these to the batting of Herbie Collins, who was to be a prolific run-getter in 1920 and 1921, and the spin bowling of Arthur Mailey, who was to take thirty-six wickets in the 1920/21 series thus breaking the Ashes record of Sydney Barnes and George Giffen, then Australia were unquestionably a powerful combination.

However, what one finds on closer examination is yet another instance in English Test cricket history where the selectors contrived to make the worst possible use of resources that were more than adequate. And, once again, the tall, unsmiling and cantankerous figure of Sydney Barnes played his customary role of "Banquo's Ghost", which he had so effectively cast for himself before the war. Plum Warner, in the Wisden of 1922, rationalises the two England defeats thus:

We had not recovered from the war of 1914-18, in which we lost such fine cricketers as Blythe, Jeeves and Booth, all killed in action. Moreover, S.F. Barnes had retired from first-class cricket and F.R.Foster had broken a leg and could not play at all. We therefore lost five bowlers during the war period.

But the fact of the matter was that Sydney Barnes did

not retire from first class cricket. Furthermore, England had many other Test-class performers to choose from, but decided to ignore the claims of players who could have altered the course of the two series. The deaths of Blythe, Jeeves and Booth, and the incapacitation of Foster, did weaken England's bowling options considerably. However, Wilfred Rhodes had seemed rejuvenated by the five-year break, topping the bowling averages in 1919 and 1920 with over 140 wickets in both seasons. Frank Woolley had a magnificent year in 1920 - with the ball as well as the bat. He took 164 wickets in the County Championship, his highest ever return and one he would never again come near to repeating, along with 1,500 runs. Johnnie Douglas was still carrying Essex. In just eighteen games in 1919 he had taken over eighty wickets and scored over eight hundred runs, whilst in 1920 he repeated his double of the 1914 season. Harry Dean, the prolific Lancashire wicket-taker with over 100 victims in 1920, showed that his pre-war form - which included a telling contribution in the Triangular Tournament - had not deserted him. Then there were the emergent talents of J.C.White of Somerset and Charlie Parker of Gloucestershire, as well as Wilson and Waddington at Yorkshire.

What of Sydney Barnes? He had continued his fruitful pursuit of victims in the Bradford League. Despite his forty-seven years he was as fit as ever in 1920, and was to carry on proving it into the 1930's. In September 1918, with the war almost at an end, he had starred in a Bradford League XI, which included several Test players, against a strong team put out by Plum Warner, who was by now a captain in the army. Wisden's report on the game testifies to Barnes' abilities remaining firmly intact: *"Barnes, owing to a bruised foot, did little bowling on the first day, but he bowled very finely in the second innings."* The *"little bowling"* Wisden speaks of amounted to two for 18 off seven overs, whilst in the second innings he took four for 24 off twelve, easily proving himself the best bowler in England.

In the four Bradford League seasons of the Great War, with most of the teams in this league strengthened by idle first class cricketers, Sydney Barnes had taken 404 wickets at the astonishingly low average of 5.17. In 1918 he took all ten wickets in an innings of a Keighley side that included Middlesex's Jack Hearne, Yorkshire's Schofield Haigh and J.H.Crawford of the famous Surrey cricketing family. Even this feat was trumped in a Priestley Cup match against Baildon Green in the same season when he smashed his highest ever score, 168. Leslie Duckworth, in his affectionate biography, 'S.F.Barnes - Master Bowler', gives some idea of the mixture of reverence and awe in which he was held during his extraordinary dominance in the Bradford League of the war years:

Saturday afternoon after Saturday afternoon found me on the Saltaire ground, or wherever they were playing away from home, hanging about the old stone pavilion, tree-backed now as it was then, hoping for a glimpse of the great man through the dressing-room window, or hovering hopefully on the fringe of pre-match practice, praying that I should have the chance of fielding the ball and throwing it back to him. Then, when the match began, I would edge my way behind the sight-screen at the end from which he was bowling so that I could watch from the best possible vantage point.

Also, he was still very much the man that Wisden was using to sell its own brand of cricket balls; this time with a large caption celebrating his tremendous performance in Johannesburg in 1913:

WONDERFUL RECORD!
17 Wickets in a Test Match
This feat was performed by S.F.Barnes of the English Team,
when visiting South Africa

Of course, it had been with their brand of cricket ball. In fact, this particular example of Wisden's reverence to the great bowler stayed in the advertisement from 1915 until 1927, when it was replaced by the team which finally won an Ashes series for England for the first time in fourteen years.

Obviously, a fit and available Sydney Barnes was a must for a tour to Australia, where he was the most prolific wicket-taker in Test history. The invitation - along with the terms - arrived, and Barnes - being Barnes - decided that they were not good enough. This time his duel with the establishment was not over the amount of money he would receive for plying his trade in Australia, nor was it the level of expenses he could expect. His demand - rejected as preposterous by the M.C.C. - was that they should pay for his wife and child to make the trip with him.

The proposition that a professional sportsman should take his or her family on a long and important engagement is rejected in the enlightened and liberal late 20th Century. It is considered distracting and an avoidable source of problems. In the immediate years after World War One - at a time when women had only just obtained the vote - the presence of wives and children on tour was only a concept in the mind of Sydney Barnes. He did not want to be parted from his family for six long months and reasoned that he would be far happier with them at his side. The establishment, checked again by another demand from the irritant Barnes, decided they could not possibly give in to this. Stalemate ensued and Barnes decided to subordinate cricket in favour of business, remaining in England for the winter of 1920/21.

Even without Barnes the tourists should never have been beaten so easily. But Dean, a proven Test performer, the promising Charlie Parker and J.C.White were not selected. The bowlers were comprehensively destroyed as Australia only failed to reach 300 before being bowled all out on one occasion. The only success was none other than Barnes' protege, Cec Parkin. When Barnes pulled out of the tour Parkin was brought in as his replacement. He had sensibly sought Barnes' advice on bowling in Australian conditions and was easily England's highest wicket-taker in the series with sixteen, including five for 60 at Adelaide. The batting should have fared better. Only Hobbs, who averaged over fifty with more than 500 runs again, and Douglas, who showed remarkable consistency by scoring 354 runs and averaging forty, coped with the spin of Mailey. Woolley and Rhodes were the biggest disappointments. The former averaged just twenty-eight with the bat and fifty-eight with the ball - almost the exact reverse of 1911/12 incidentally - whilst the latter barely averaged twenty-three with the bat and over sixty with ball. Moreover, the selectors had overlooked Philip Mead and George Gunn, who were rivalled only by Hobbs for the volume of runs scored in the County Championships of 1919 and 1920. A.C.Russell, Harry Makepeace and Patsy Hendren, despite an occasionally inspired performance, were generally disappointing.

Perhaps it is not surprising that this team achieved such dismal results. For its captain was - once again - Johnnie Won't Hit Today Douglas, able this time to indulge himself in the role of strike bowler, and found wanting in every respect as his eight wickets at over fifty apiece prove. The situation undoubtedly called out for the class of Sydney Barnes. But he was running a small business in Wales, enjoying a comfortable living as a member of the labour aristocracy with his wife and child to provide succour on those dark, cold winter nights. If he reflected on the fate of the England team in Australia - which is doubtful - it would have been merely to rue the loss of a hat-full of batsmen, snared in his expert trap.

In the summer of 1921 the selectors prevaricated and blustered to such an extent that no less than thirty players and two captains were used. The committee, consisting of Reggie Spooner, who had declined the captaincy for the tour of 1920/21 thus leaving Douglas to claim his rightful place in Test cricket history, John Daniell, the captain and mainstay of Somerset, and H.K.Foster, one of the famous Worcestershire brothers, contrived to make some yearn for the faulty but decisive logic of Lord Hawke. Philip Mead was ignored until the final two Tests, despite performing prolific feats in the County Championship of 1921. When he was eventually chosen he showed the selectors the folly of their ways by scoring 229 runs for once out. George Gunn was completely neglected. The batting, apart from Woolley, Tennyson - who replaced Douglas as captain by the third Test - and Russell, failed miserably. Of this trio only Woolley played in all the Tests, whilst Jack Hobbs was sick and unable to play all summer. The claims of the Yorkshire opening pair of Holmes and Sutcliffe were largely disregarded. The bowling was just as pitiful as on the tour, Cec Parkin once again being leading wicket-taker with sixteen from only four Tests.

Amongst the unedifying spectacles of the summer were the selectors' inquiring as to the temperament of various candidates from casual spectators, the summoning of Tennyson to captain the side at one o'clock on the morning of the third Test when he was in his club and rather the worse for drink, and the sight of the Australian skipper, Warwick Armstrong, reading a newspaper on the boundary at the Oval as the final Test petered out into a draw. His explanation? He was trying to find out who they were playing!

The ultimate irony came at Eastbourne in August. This magnificent unbeaten Australian team were humbled by a scratch eleven selected and captained by none other than Archibald Campbell MacLaren, who was now in his fiftieth year. *"I think I know how to beat Armstrong's lot,"* he had boasted to Neville Cardus in a letter to the offices of the

Manchester Guardian, whilst urging the paper's cricket correspondent to attend this historic match. Ignoring his Editor, who had wanted him to be at the Oval for the crucial Surrey versus Yorkshire fixture, Cardus travelled to the south coast merely to please his childhood hero. *"I achieved this, the only scoop of my career,"* Cardus was to explain repeatedly over the years as he recalled the miracle that he had witnessed.

MacLaren's victory was gained by the virtue of bowling a good line and length; exactly an attribute - along with many others - of Sydney Barnes. It seems that Barnes was the one professional in England who was ignored in 1921. His failure to accept the invitation to go to Australia in 1920/21 meant - to the gentlemanly cricket establishment - that he had *"retired"* of his own accord. Perhaps it was also felt that he was too old. If this was true then it merely serves to show the stupidity of the selectors - and not only because of his performances in Minor Counties cricket in the 1920's and 30's. English cricket history is littered with examples of experienced players, almost as old as Sydney Barnes in 1921, returning to Test cricket and performing heroics. The most famous example is that of Wilfred Rhodes, who was forty-eight years old - the same age as Barnes in 1921 - when he was recalled against Australia at the Oval in 1926 to make a decisive contribution in the winning of the Ashes for the first time in fourteen years. Rhodes was still playing in Test matches after his fiftieth birthday, as were W.G.Grace and George Gunn. Hobbs and Woolley played their last Tests when they were forty-seven; Strudwick and Hendren forty-six. The most famous recent example was Brian Close's selection to face the might of the West Indian pace attack in 1976 at Old Trafford at forty-five years of age.

The only player in England who had proved he could change the course of - or even win - a series by himself was totally ignored, much to the detriment of English cricket.

Sydney Barnes disappeared from the limelight, playing for Saltaire in the Bradford League until, in 1924, at the age of fifty-one, he resumed his career with Staffordshire and became the most prolific performer the Minor Counties Championship has ever seen.

14.

BARNES OF STAFFORDSHIRE

The return of the fifty-one year old Sydney Barnes to the Staffordshire team after a ten year break had a galvanising effect on team morale and results - just has it had done when he first appeared for the county twenty years earlier. William Gatus Watson, in his 1923 book 'Staffordshire Cricket', wrote: *"Barnes was a great acquisition to the club in all departments of the game."* In fact, as the greatest cricketer that had ever played for the county he was known, quite simply, as the *"maestro"*.

Of all the counties taking part in the minor championship it has always been something of a surprise that Staffordshire, considering its size, has not graduated to the full County Championship. As a fairly large county, with Wolverhampton to the south, Stoke-on-Trent in the north and the county town of Stafford in the centre, it seems to have the perfect population base to support a first class county. But it is its geography that has prevented the transition. Staffordshire is shaped rather like a dumb-bell, and the area between the two major centres of population in the north and south is sparsely inhabited. Moreover, Wolverhampton is demographically connected with Birmingham and the Midlands, with the major league teams in the area playing in the Birmingham League and thus providing players for Warwickshire and Worcestershire. Sydney Barnes' home-town club, Smethwick, still plays in the Birmingham League even though it is in Staffordshire. Cricket in Staffordshire, therefore, centred around Stoke-on-Trent and the Potteries and most of its players were members of teams in the North Staffordshire League.

When Sydney Barnes began his long career with Staffordshire, which was to encompass twenty-two seasons over thirty years, the county had never won the Minor Counties Championship and had finished the 1903 season fourth from bottom. Albert Hollowood, father of Bernard, was the county's leading batsman and had also topped the bowling averages in that season with six wickets for 49 runs. Inevitably, the acquisition of a bowler of the class of Barnes, who had just taken 131 wickets in a County Championship season and had claimed twenty-six victims in only four Tests, would see a remarkable transformation in the fortunes of this previously under-achieving county.

However, the metamorphosis did not happen overnight. Even though Barnes began in the manner in which he was to continue, effortlessly picking up victims at minimal cost, the county made only limited progress at first. In that 1904 season, as Staffordshire moved up to seventh place in the championship, Barnes took 66 wickets at just over ten runs apiece. In his very first game he took eleven wickets for 134 runs against a Northamptonshire side which was soon to become the sixteenth first class county. It was a good start to his minor counties career and would have been much better but for the fact that he sustained yet another injury, straining his side, and was unable to bowl in the last five games. During this period he was played as a batsman until, in a game against Dorset at Poole, he made a dramatic recovery and gave an insight into his growing genius. Barnes himself takes up the story:

Dorset batted first and though the wicket was one of the stickiest I have ever seen they were scoring very easily. None of our bowlers could take advantage of the conditions, so I told H.D.Stratton, our

S. F. BARNES
Staffordshire

captain, that if he would send someone into the town for a plaster I would strap up my side and see if I could manage to bowl without running up to the wicket. By the time the plaster had arrived and I had strapped up the score stood at 110 for two, not bad on a sticky wicket. I took over the bowling and got the remaining eight wickets for 10 runs!

The next season he did not perform nearly so well, taking just forty-four wickets at a cost of 11.54; a superb performance for any ordinary seam bowler but undoubtedly disappointing to a perfectionist such as Sydney Barnes. Furthermore, he seems to have received something of a going over when playing against some of the minor counties in the south of England, a blow to his pride unquestionably. As Wisden reports: *"Barnes and Mee did practically all the bowling, but if they had not been so freely hit during the Southern tour their records would have been even better."*

What changed in 1906 - and was to give Barnes renewed impetus - was the ending of his association with the Lancashire League and his return to live in the county of his birth and play his league cricket for Porthill Park in the North Staffordshire League. Although he had enjoyed his years in the Lancashire League, with Rishton, Burnley and then Church for the previous two seasons, he no doubt found the constant travelling dissatisfactory and wanted to concentrate his energies on reviving the fortunes of Staffordshire. The competitiveness of the Lancashire League had taught him a lot; it had made him a well-known cricketer, but it was now time to find pastures new and help his home county and league raise its standards.

In 1906, as Staffordshire marched triumphantly to their first ever Minor Counties title, Sydney Barnes created a record which may never be broken. Bowling 373.1 overs, a hundred of which were maidens, he took no fewer than 119 wickets at an average of 7.83. It was an incredible accomplishment and is fourteen wickets more than the next best performance in that particular championship, both before and since. At this point in his career Wisden becomes gushing in its praise: *"What lent distinction to a highly successful season was the wonderfully fine bowling of Barnes,"* it enthuses. Little wonder, considering some of his brilliant bowling: eight for 10 in one innings against Bedfordshire, fifteen for 93 and fourteen for 72 in the matches against Cambridgeshire and Suffolk, and twelve for 88 against a strong Yorkshire 2nd XI, are achievements of the highest calibre. Wisden refers to him as *"the old Lancashire cricketer"*, amusing in hindsight when one considers that he was still playing for Staffordshire nearly thirty years later.

What Barnes also revealed in 1906, which apart from one or two instances had hitherto remained hidden, were his abilities as a batsman. At Test level he was often accused of throwing his wicket away. *"Why don't you try to make runs?"* C.B.Fry once asked. *"If I make a century and took no wickets, would the selectors pick me for my batting?"* was his typical response. Nevertheless, he was good enough to make a score of 93 in one England tour game. He made his first century in that 1906 championship-winning season, and went on to score 431 runs at an average of over thirty. He undoubtedly revelled in his new role as an all-rounder, entering the fray in the middle-order and smashing some quick runs. In 1904 he had immediately announced his credentials as a batsman by scoring 455 runs at an average of thirty-five, and throughout his Staffordshire career he was to be remarkably consistent. His best seasons with the bat were to be in 1911, when he scored 563 runs and averaged 43.3 including an innings of 150, and 1913, when he again averaged over 40. In the former season he also created a world record against Durham at South Shields when he scored 136 with the bat and took seventeen wickets for 83 with the ball.

For the 1907 season the Minor Counties Championship was re-organised into four regional divisions. The competition had grown to more than twenty counties, which was deemed to be too many for every side to play each other because of the travelling and the vagaries of the weather. The winners of each section were to play semi-finals and a final at the end of the season. It was Staffordshire's misfortune to be in the same group as a very strong Lancashire 2nd XI in 1907. They were pipped for top position by Lancashire - who went on to easily carry off the title - by the narrowest of margins, and would almost certainly have won had the game between the two not been abandoned because of the weather. Wisden gives another reason for Staffordshire's failure to win their section: *"Barnes was in excellent bowling form...but his batting fell off."* His seventy-nine wickets cost only 6.39 each but, for only the second time before the First World War, his batting average fell below twenty.

His performances in 1906 and 1907 no doubt led to his inclusion in the England touring party to Australia. Having enhanced his reputation in Australia, he returned to Staffordshire the following season to guide them to their second title triumph in only three years. His ninety-two wickets at 8.88 made them comfortable winners of the Northern section, and they easily beat Glamorgan, who were embarking on their own progress towards first class status, in the final. At this point Wisden hints, in the hope unquestionably of getting Barnes back into the County Championship, for Staffordshire to move up a grade: *"They showed brilliant form all the summer, and thanks to Barnes they were a really fine eleven - well able to hold their own in even better company."*

If the prospect of becoming a first class county was discussed in Staffordshire, then if anybody had asked Sydney Barnes for his opinion it would certainly have been a curt negative. Barnes was content to wheel away for Porthill Park at the weekend and play two-day county games in a

155

competition he was able to dominate without having to stretch himself too much. Now he was back in the England team he could reserve his best for the Tests and the major representative fixtures. He was more than happy - and so were Staffordshire - even though it was another three years before they again won the Minor Counties championship.

Restricted to fewer appearances in 1909, due to Test match calls and other games, Barnes still took seventy-six wickets at a miserly 6.77. However, he had his most disappointing season with the bat, barely scratching together one hundred runs at an average little above twelve. Nevertheless, it was this season that he produced his most startling bowling analysis. Against Cheshire at Stoke he took fourteen wickets for an astonishing thirteen runs. In the first innings he had taken eight for six off 11.5 overs, and in the second he added six more wickets for seven off 8.4 overs. It is one of the most amazing statistics in cricket history. Furthermore, in the 1910 edition of Wisden, to supplement the honour of being one of the Five Cricketers of the Year, the role he had played in heightening the profile of Staffordshire cricket was recognised: *"Once more the chief man of their eleven was Barnes, who by being picked to play for England, conferred distinction upon his county."*

Staffordshire had their least successful season since Barnes' arrival in 1910, but Sydney Barnes was just as prolific. His ninety wickets cost just under ten apiece and his batting form returned as he scored over 300 runs and averaged over twenty. They slipped to fifth in a combined North and East Division, which was a prelude to the return of a single division in 1912. If their rivals felt that Staffordshire's stranglehold on the championship was loosening they were to be sadly mistaken. In 1911 Barnes and Staffordshire dominated the last season of inter-divisional cricket. They romped home in the North and East Division and then massacred Surrey 2nd XI by 334 runs in the final in September.

As well as his 563 runs - including two centuries - he claimed 104 victims with his special brand of bowling, at a cost of 7.21 apiece. In the final, as well as contributing a gritty thirty-six in the second innings on a treacherous wicket, he took ten wickets in the match for only 74 runs. On top of this, he mesmerised the touring All-India team at Stoke by taking fourteen wickets for a mere 29 runs. It was superb preparation for the havoc he was about to wreak in Australia on the forthcoming tour.

Widely acclaimed as the best bowler in the world, he still managed to appear regularly for Staffordshire in the damp summer of 1912, despite the added distraction of the Triangular Tournament. He was practically unplayable this year and his seventy wickets cost just over five runs apiece. Even though they remained unbeaten all season, Staffordshire finished as runners-up to Norfolk, whom they had beaten in their only meeting. With four matches abandoned due to rain and Sydney Barnes missing some key fixtures, the return of the single division format had worked against them. Despite Barnes' wickets, sixty-five at 6.10, and runs, 366 at 40.66, Staffordshire fell to fourth behind Norfolk in 1913. At forty years of age in 1913, Barnes performed a unique double. As well as topping the minor counties averages for the sixth time in ten years, he led the first class figures as well. It was a feat which he was to repeat, remarkably, fifteen years later. Officially they are not credited as champions in 1914, even though they were top of the table when the competition was brought to a close with the advent of war. Sydney Barnes was having another prolific season when the championship was terminated and it seemed that, at forty-one years of age, his Staffordshire days were over.

Why did he remain so loyal to Staffordshire cricket when he quite palpably did not with Lancashire - and even with England! The answer, of course, lies partly in the format of the Minor Counties Championship. One two-day game a week, plus a league match at the weekend, suited him physically. His numerous injuries showed the strain bowling placed on his body, and there is no doubt that had he played county cricket right up to the war he would have burned himself out like so many others. Certainly, he would not still have been playing for Staffordshire at the age of sixty-one had he not looked after his physique in the way that gentlemen amateurs who captained county teams would not. However, it seems that of all the teams he played for it was the administrators and captains of Staffordshire who treated him the best. Bernard Hollowood makes this interesting assertion:

He had less trouble, and caused less trouble, with his native Staffordshire than in any other cricket, chiefly because the county treated him well and was fortunate enough to have officials - presidents, secretaries and captains - who understood him and knew how to humour him. I do not mean that Duncan Stratton, Bernard Meakin, J.B.Russell and Stanley Heath were lenient with him and submitted to his petulance and abrasiveness: only that each of these captains in his own way took the trouble to comprehend Barnes's motivation and moods and acquired the knack of removing his sting.

There was no great surprise therefore - at least not in Staffordshire - when the fifty-one year old Sydney Barnes returned to the fold in 1924 when the county's form and fortune had dipped. Having won the first two post-war championships, in 1920 and 1921, they had a disastrous 1922, winning only two games, and, although they climbed to fifth in 1923, they were clearly a team in decline. In its report on the county's 1924 season, Wisden defines the impact of his return clearly and concisely: *"Easily the outstanding feature of Staffordshire cricket last season was the splendid bowling of Sidney Barnes."* He had taken seventy-three wickets at 7.17 runs apiece - not bad for an old has-been!

The following season many felt Barnes was on his way out. It was his least successful season ever for Staffordshire, taking only thirty-one wickets at the remarkably high average - for him at least - of 13.45. Wisden hints at the possible end to a truly great career: *"S.F.Barnes, though bowling well, did not meet with such extraordinary success as in 1924."* It was at this time as well that Barnes disappears from Wisden's advertisement for their brand of cricket balls. But, yet again, Wisden had acted with an indecent haste unbecoming of such an authoritative tome. If the Editors of the cricket bible had ever thought of eating their product - as opposed to their hats - then Barnes' performance in 1926 should have given them the perfect incentive. His seventy-six wickets at 8.21 apiece, including a brilliant fourteen for 31 against Lincolnshire, was his best return since that great season of 1911. Wisden, as a form of apologia, salutes the master bowler and his Staffordshire career:

The feature of the season's work was the wonderful success of Barnes, who, heading the bowling averages once again, despite his 50 years, brought his total of wickets in the course of fourteen seasons to 1,050 for 7.98 runs each.

This particular Wisden eulogy demonstrates one of the great mysteries of Sydney Barnes' life. Up until this period of his career his date of birth in Wisden had been listed as occurring in 1876. Instead of being fifty years of age in 1926, as Wisden so proudly boasts, he was, in fact, fifty-three, making his performance that season all the more remarkable. This particular mystery was only cleared up by Wisden in 1930, when it finally reproduced the great man's correct date of birth.

By 1927, however, Barnes' return had not helped Staffordshire to improve their position in the championship. They had finished seventh in 1924 and 1926 and even lower in 1925, when Barnes had had such a poor season by his standards. Admittedly, they had been unlucky not to win more games in 1924 because three of their opponents managed to save the follow-on by a single run. In 1927 all that was to change as they stormed to their sixth title in little over twenty years to make them the most successful minor county of the period. Inevitably it was Barnes, of whom Wisden says *"proved the deciding factor in closely-contested games"*, who delivered Staffordshire another great triumph. The statistics tell the story: fourteen for 52 against Leicestershire 2nd XI at Wolverhampton, ten for 66 in the return at Loughborough, thirteen for 62 against Nottinghamshire 2nd XI at his old home ground of Porthill Park, eleven for 46 against Lancashire 2nd XI at Stoke and seven for 19 in one innings against Lincolnshire at Frodingham. He claimed eighty-one victims at little more than six apiece. To the complete amazement of the cricket world, a fifty-four year old medium-fast bowler had shown that he was still one of the finest performers in the game.

Over the next five seasons Staffordshire did not scale the heights which they had reached in 1927; but Sydney Barnes continued taking wickets. In 1928 there were fifty-five at 7.34, including nine for 63 at Grimsby against Lincolnshire and fifteen for 67 at Porthill Park against Cheshire. His sixty-eight wickets at 8.3 in 1929 made up for his poor batting form. In 1930, however, he corrected that by topping the batting averages with 252 runs at an average of 31.5, as well as claiming fifty-one wickets at 5.74, his second lowest average. In one innings against Lancashire 2nd XI he produced the superb figures of eleven overs, seven wickets, including those of Eddie Paynter and Bill Farrimond, two players who were later to star at Test level, for a mere twenty runs. Bernard Hollowood played in this game and remembers meeting Paynter, Farrimond, Reg Parkin and Harry Butterworth at a fairground that evening.

160

"Well, well," exclaimed Hollowood. *"I should have thought you'd all be in bed, instead of gadding about. You've got another dose of Barney tomorrow."*

"But we're celebrating," replied Reg Parkin. *"Harry, here, considers his innings the best he's ever played."*

Paynter was later to vividly recall that game and Sydney Barnes' part in it. He had wanted to have a look behind the bowler's arm at this ancient bowler his team mates had talked about before arriving at the ground. His captain had ordered him to put his pads on even though he was batting at number six. *"And there were four of us,"* exclaimed the amazed Paynter, *"all padded up and waiting. And we were all out in the middle and back again in half an hour!"*

Wisden, in its review of Staffordshire's 1931 season, gives an inkling as to the fifty-eight year old's supreme skill when it says: *"In one innings he sent down 85 balls, only three of which were scored from."* In 1932 he added fifty-one wickets to his sixty-one of the previous year. His wickets were still costing less than ten runs apiece, and the ultimate irony came at Stoke that year when he produced the remarkable return of thirteen for 50 against a Lancashire 2nd XI, some of whom he had been tutoring as a Lancashire coach at the time.

In 1933 he was sixty years old - a phenomenal age for a fast bowler - and it was obvious that his career was coming to an end. He concentrated on his duties as professional with Rawtenstall and played just three games for Staffordshire. The changing cricket world could not have been exemplified more to the prehistoric Barnes than with the vilification of the returning England touring team after the notorious "Bodyline" series in Australia. As an extremely aggressive cricketer, who had been garlanded in Australia for his tremendous feats, he must surely have produced a wry smile on hearing of the antics of Douglas Jardine and his fast bowlers. He would certainly have balked at the use of leg theory. He didn't need it. Nevertheless, a man as crassly competitive as Douglas Jardine - even though he was a gentleman amateur - would have appealed to the character of Sydney Francis Barnes.

Those three games in 1933 yielded only seven wickets. For the first time since his return to the Staffordshire side in 1924 he dropped out of the Minor Counties bowling averages. In fact, he had headed those averages on four occassions, finished second three times to bowlers who had taken considerably fewer wickets, and third once. Only in 1925, when he had had such a poor season, did he finish out of the top three. It would have been a startling statistic for someone in their prime, but for a bowler for whom those years encompassed a sixth decade it is truly phenomenal.

By 1935, however, the writing was on the wall. Wisden reported that Barnes *"concluded his career with the county after the first two matches"*. Not for the first time Wisden erred. In 1935 he added a further nine wickets to his impressive career total. He now realised that it was time for him to call it a day. In twenty-two seasons with Staffordshire he had taken 1,441wickets at a cost of 8.15 runs per wicket. It was - and still is - the most prolific bowling career the Minor Counties Championship has ever seen.

15.

SWANSONG

Bernard Hollowood played a supporting role in the final act of Sydney Barnes' representative career:

I was batting with him in his last match for Staffordshire at Castleford in 1935 when he was given out, LBW, to the Yorkshire fast bowler, Hargreaves. From the other end he looked dead in front, but Barnes stood his ground and glowered at the umpire for so long that I honestly thought he had refused to go. The fielders watched, immobile and fascinated, and the umpire looked distinctly uncomfortable. Then, with the passing of aeons, old Syd turned and marched to the pavilion with a face like that of Mr Hyde.

It would be a remarkably poignant image to end the cricket career of Sydney Barnes in this way: once again in conflict with the authorities as he makes his final departure from the cricket world at the grand old age of sixty-two. But, as one would expect of a genius whose achievements against all the odds speak for themselves, this was never ordained to be his final bow on the cricket field. For, until 1940, he continued to play league cricket with the success that had followed him around throughout his career.

His last season for Saltaire was in 1923. He had been living in Colwyn Bay in North Wales where he had a small business, but his wife fell ill and he was forced to move back to Staffordshire, one reason why he resumed playing for his

163

'Barnes (S. F.) lbw b Hargreaves . . .'

native county. The club he chose to join in 1924 was Castleton Moor in the Central Lancashire League. This particular league was no poor relation to either the Lancashire League or the Bradford League. Formed in the same year as the powerful Lancashire League, the cricket was every bit as competitive and most of the clubs were affluent enough to afford at least one professional. Even nowadays this league still attracts a plentiful supply of overseas players, many of them Test stars in their own right. Castleton Moor, however, until the arrival of Barnes, were one of the league's poor relations.

Having finished in tenth place (out of twelve) in 1922 and 1923, they rose to fifth in 1924 as Barnes took ninety wickets at 6.45. The next four years saw Castleton Moor scale heights undreamt of in the club's pre-Barnes existence. By 1926 they were league champions. Disappointed by finishing as runners-up in 1927 they exceeded all their expectations the following year when they won both the league and the Wood Cup. Inevitably, it was Barnes who delivered those triumphs. After 1924 he passed 100 wickets for the season in each of the other four years, totalling 583 wickets in all for Castleton Moor at an average of 5.98. Sydney Barnes had, for the umpteenth time, turned a mediocre team into a match for all its rivals.

Amazingly, Castleton Moor were then forced to release him because they could no longer afford to pay him the money he required. Barnes had wanted a two-year contract at £450 a year but the club was unable to obtain enough financial guarantees from its members so, reluctantly, he departed. The Mayor of Castleton Moor made a speech at the committee meeting in which his services were dispensed with which clearly gives an insight into the high esteem and affection in which he was held both on and off the field:

No professional has enthused such loyalty into his players as Barnes has done in the last two or three years. I wish to kill once and for all the notion which seems to have been broadcast during the last few years that Barnes is a bad man to get on with. He is a very reticent man, and like all geniuses he has his own way of doing things, but he is certainly not difficult to get on with; the boys adore him and will be very sorry indeed if he goes elsewhere.

Castleton Moor's loss was Rochdale's gain. Rochdale Cricket Club, one of the cricketing and financial powerhouses of the Central Lancashire League, signed him up for the next two seasons when he added another 203 wickets at 7.32 to his remarkable figures in league cricket. Leslie Duckworth recounts a wonderful story about Barnes at Rochdale. Playing against bottom-of-the-table Walsden one beautiful June day Barnes was ripping through the opposition with ease when a Walsden third-teamer, making up the numbers, strolled out and promptly dispatched the great man for four consecutive boundaries, returning to the pavilion to a standing ovation:

'Well played, lad,' said his captain. *'Do you know who t' bowler is?'*
'Nay, ah don't,' the lad replied.
'Well, it wor Syd Barnes,' the captain told him.
'Well, all ah can say,' the lad retorted, *'is that ah wish he'd bin on at both ends.'*

From Rochdale it was back to the Lancashire League with Rawtenstall where his first season saw him take 115 wickets at 6.30, the lowest average in that club's history. He passed 100 wickets again the following year before disappointing a little in 1933 with only fifty-four wickets at 13.72, although for much of the 1933 season he was suffering from a knee injury. It was during this period that he was to have his classic confrontations with the great West Indian Learie Constantine, who was, along with his journalist compatriot C.L.R.James, providing the world with news of the magnificent cricket being played in the Lancashire League. This report of a game between Constantine's club, Nelson, and Rawtenstall, penned by James, appeared in the Manchester Guardian in 1932:

Barnes took 7 wickets for 30 runs, aided no doubt by the terror of his name. When Constantine came in I looked for a duel. Constantine was not going to be drawn into playing forward. Barnes was not going to bowl short. Constantine was not going to chance it. So the pair watched each other like two fencers sparring for an opening. The crowd sat tense, was this recitative suddenly to burst into a melody of fours and sixes? The Nelson crowd at least hoped so, but it was not to be. Some insignificant trundler at the other end who bowled mediocre balls, bowled Constantine with one of them... When Barnes came in, Constantine was hurling the ball violently through the air, Barnes was older than Constantine's father and the wicket was faster now. He judged the ball quickly and got there in time. His bones were too stiff to force the ball away, but his bat swung true to the drive and he got over the ball to cut. He stayed there some forty minutes for 10 and as long as he was there his side was winning. But Constantine bowled him behind his back. He came in slowly amidst the plaudits of the Nelson crowd, applauding his innings and their satisfaction at him having been dismissed. Courtesy acknowledged the applause. After he left, Rawtenstall collapsed.

With his career at Staffordshire drawing to a close it seemed as though retirement should have been the order of the day for the ancient Sydney Barnes. As he played fewer and fewer games for his county in 1933, 1934 and 1935 many talked of his *"decline in form"* as if it was due to some other reason than the fact that he was now well into his sixties. Some commentators were, quite simply, amazed that Staffordshire could drop him as, on his day, he was still a great bowler. In fact, from 1934 until 1940 time and again he

167

proved in league cricket that there was and would never be a substitute for guile, length and line. In 1934 he signed for Keighley in the Bradford League and treated the aficionados of that league to a virtuoso season, reminding many of his magnificent nine-year spell at Saltaire. He bowled no fewer than 413.4 overs during that season, 122 of which were maidens and his eighty-six wickets cost 10.36 apiece, only the fourth time in thirty-eight seasons of league cricket that his average had reached double figures.

From Keighley he returned full circle, to his home-town club of Smethwick in the Birmingham League, for two wonderful seasons. In 1935 he took seventy-five wickets at an average of 8.65. Some of his magnificent performances are well worth recording: five for 26 against West Bromich Dartmouth, seven for 49 against Aston Unity, a magnificent nine for 40 against Dudley, four for 9 against Moseley with eight for 52 in the return, five for 12 against Stourbridge, six for 30 against Walsall and six for 29 against Mitchell and Butlers. The club's report on the season contained the following remarks:

Had our batting showed the same stability that our bowling showed keenness, there is little doubt that our ambition (to win the championship - they finished third) *would at last have been realised. Tommy Durnell and Barnes were in magnificent form with the ball, the latter displaying all the guile that made him so famous a bowler and the former revealing tremendous speed and accuracy. On no fewer than five occasions they bowled throughout the innings unchanged...The gate receipts were up and this counterbalances the extra amount paid in wages. In fact, it can be said that our venture in engaging Sydney Barnes as professional was quite justified.*

The latter comments show that even though he was now well advanced in years Sydney Barnes could still negotiate a mean contract. Naturally, Barnes had asked Smethwick to pay him more than they could afford, but the master bowler had assured his new employers that his appearance for his home-town team was guaranteed to significantly improve the attendances and thus the gate money. As well as a fee he also received a share of the gate receipts and this arrangement must have been a success as he was re-engaged for the following season. His haul of only thirty-eight wickets at 11.52 in 1936 was disappointing, but Durnell, his opening partner, who had finished below Barnes in the averages in 1935 with sixty-nine wickets at 10.48, gives a good reason why his follow-up season was not as productive when he says: *"he was the greatest controlled bowler I ever saw. When the sun had warmed his hands and loosened the muscles he was at his best. On a cold day he suffered badly and could do little with the ball."* 1936 was a very wet and cold summer, which accounts for his moderate figures, but, as usual, there were some stunning returns: seven for 23 against Kidderminster, five for 30 against West Bromich Dartmouth and five for 30 again against Stourbridge. Durnell, incidentally, managed just thirty-four wickets himself in 1936.

Despite the fact that he was not re-appointed for the 1937 season he was still made an honourary life member of the club and Smethwick remain proud of his association with them. Instead, he played in yet another competition, the Ribblesdale League, for the St Anne's club which is now a member of the strong Northern League. During that season he bowled an astonishing 516.2 overs, conceding his runs at less than one and a half an over and taking sixty-one wickets at 12.47 apiece. At the same time other cricket luminaries were playing for teams in the Ribblesdale League. Ted McDonald, the tremendous Australian fast bowler and the Lancashire League's first *"sensation signing"*, Barnes' post-war protege Cec Parkin, and the New Zealanders Dempster and James, all played for various clubs in the Ribble Valley, showing that Barnes had chosen no easy option. Again gate receipts improved and Sydney Barnes created a favourable impression in spite of what one club member recounts as *"the dressing-room ritual of rubbing down before and after with a very strong-smelling embrocation."*

In 1938 Barnes played for Bridgnorth, the club with whom Cyril Washbrook first found fame, in Shropshire. Although they did not play in any league they had a superb fixture list and for the last time in Sydney Barnes' league career he was to take over 100 wickets in a season. At the age of sixty-five he took 126 wickets at 6.94 apiece and topped the batting averages as well for good measure with a serene 28.55 per innings. Even though the cricket was not quite up to the standard of the previous few years it was, nevertheless, a quite amazing accomplishment for a man of such an advanced age.

A truly astonishing statistic is that the season of 1939, the year of the outbreak of the Second World War, was the first season since 1895 that Sydney Barnes did not have a professional contract. His hopes, maybe, of a peaceful retirement were put on hold in 1940 when Sir Ernest Johnson of the Stone Cricket Club in the North Staffordshire and South Cheshire League persuaded him to coach at the club and play a few games. He appeared in seventeen matches, bowling in twelve. Amongst the miraculous performances churned out by this formidable individual were six for 32 away at Great Chell in the first game, five for 43 at home to Leek in the second, five for 22 at Caverswell and four for 12 off fourteen overs in the return at Great Chell. He had a top score of thirty-eight at Stone against Blythe Colour Works, finishing with 191 runs at an average of 11.93. His twenty-eight wickets cost just 8.28 apiece and his final wicket in league cricket came at the ground of the Blythe Colour Works. It was his 6,229th wicket as a professional cricketer.

16.

THE RELUCTANT CELEBRITY

Sydney Barnes began his exceptional impact on international cricket with Europe beginning its descent towards a disastrous war; he retired from active participation in cricket with a conflict of an even more global and destructive nature having already commenced. The development of mass communications and the arrival of new generations of citizens unwilling to accept the status quo promoted a reappraisal of history. Consequently, the exploits of Sydney Barnes, who had always felt himself to be under-valued and lacking in recognition, were seen in a different light.

Whereas the Victorian and Edwardian generation of commentators would have admired a player's prowess on the field but deplored his social skills, a new era ushered in a desire for more egalitarianism. People were coming to the conclusion that a meritocracy was far more desirable than a system based on class and privilege. Solid achievement was now to be proof of ability rather than glorious failure. No longer would an amateur cricketer - who had promised much but delivered briefly - be regarded as superior to the grafting professional whose consistency over two decades had given stability and growth. The major beneficiary of the re-assessment of cricket history was Sydney Francis Barnes. For, towards the end of Barnes' cricket career, two phenomena appeared in the world of international cricket which enabled

S. F. BARNES

the game to begin to shake itself out of its social torpor. Firstly, the previously nepotic world of Test cricket expanded its horizons. Although South Africa had been involved in official Tests since 1888, only for a few short years did they compete with something like parity before the First World War. By the late 1920's and early 1930's they began winning Test matches and series on a regular basis. Furthermore, the cricket family expanded to reflect its global appeal. In 1928, England gave Test status to games with the West Indies, in 1929 New Zealand, and in 1932 India. This democratisation of cricket saw the search for comparison with other generations. When it came to bowling these new members needed only glance into the records of Wisden to find the greatest performer in history with which to measure the successes of their own players. The name they would come up with was that of Sydney Francis Barnes.

Barnes competed against these new members of cricket's global family with outstanding success. Playing for North Wales against the visiting South Africans in 1924 he took five wickets for just 32 runs from sixteen overs. One of his victims was none other than the great Herbie Taylor, dismissed cheaply, much to Barnes' obvious satisfaction. He trumped that when the South Africans visited again in 1929, this time for the full Wales team. In the first innings he had the memorable figures of eight for 41, and total match figures of nine for 60. In 1927 he grabbed four for 47 from no less than thirty-five overs against the touring New Zealanders, adding a further three victims against them for Staffordshire in 1931. Against the All India team in 1932, some twenty years after his fourteen for 29 and in his sixtieth year, his match figures were an impressive thirty-nine overs, five wickets for 85 runs.

Secondly, the appearance of Donald Bradman, with his prolific and consistent run-scoring, engendered a crusade which has famously been termed, *"The Battle to Get Bradman Out"*. As bowler after bowler were flayed mercilessly around the Test cricket grounds of Australia and England from 1928 onwards, experts searched for an answer to the Bradman conundrum. Bodyline served only to curtail his activities temporarily; a definitive response was needed. History confirms that no bowler managed to dominate the Don, but the media were in no doubt - based on all available evidence - that Sydney Francis Barnes was the only man capable of competing on equal terms.

As a result, Barnes became a celebrity of immense proportions. In truth, he had never really disappeared from the public eye. His return to the Staffordshire team in 1924 had created a mythology all of its own, and even those who had previously lambasted Barnes for his behaviour and disloyalty during the Edwardian era were forced to revise their opinions. He proved the inspiration for old masters as well as promising youngsters. John Tyldesley, the only professional batsman to gain a regular England place in the Golden Age, appeared for Lancashire 2nd XI against the rejuvenated Staffordshire in 1926. *"I thought my days of scoring centuries were over, but I'm going to get one against him,"* determined the great batsman, who was even older than the Staffordshire veteran. He proceeded to score 127 in two and a half hours.

In 1929, Lancashire, the dominant county side of the period, entertained a Minor Counties representative side including, naturally, the fifty-three year old Sydney Barnes as the bowling spearhead. On a wonderful batsman's wicket he still managed to bowl :

with his sixth delivery, take a slip catch and finish with two for 98. His second victim was Harry Makepeace, who had hit a majestic seventy. Barnes lured him into an injudicious stroke when he had looked well set for a century. The Manchester Guardian commented that it was *"the fowler snaring the old and crafty bird"*. Undoubtedly, it was this performance which prompted Lancashire to employ Barnes as a bowling coach at Old Trafford. At his side was his old mentor, Archie MacLaren; two classical performers of the Golden Age in tandem. Their example saw a new generation of Lancashire players emerge to continue the county's success into the 1930's.

A famous story sees Sydney Barnes arrive at Old Trafford in April of 1933 for pre-season practice. As he left his train he was approached by a callow eighteen-year-old asking directions to the Old Trafford ground. *"What are you, a batsman or a bowler?"* grunted the surly old-timer in the hope that the youngster's response might enable him to fulminate on his craft. *"There's not much chance for batsmen here,"* replied Barnes sharply when the young man admitted he was the old master's foe rather than friend. This anecdote would be of little interest but for the fact that the aspiring batsman was none other than Cyril Washbrook, who was to be another great international cricketer overlapping a world war, and yet another example of the way Barnes the man was to slip easily into cricket folklore.

The fame of Sydney Barnes was to spread further and wider than it had done throughout his playing career. In 1928 he had played for Wales against the first touring West Indian side accorded Test status. In a display which completely astonished his calypso-inspired opponents, Barnes took twelve wickets for 118 runs in the match. George Challenor, whose performances on this tour made him the first great West Indian batsman, commented: *"I simply couldn't guess as the ball floated fairly quickly to the pitch what it was going to do - leg or off spin."* A team which had only recently absorbed the lessons of patience and control to ally with flair and exuberance had been decimated by the epitome of the perfect mixture of those two disciplines. This performance enabled Barnes to top the first class bowling averages for the second time that year. In 1929 he was to finish fifth. His final game against overseas opposition was against the West Indies tourists of 1933. Even though his abilities were on the wane and he claimed no wickets, he still managed five maidens in eight overs of controlled medium pace.

C.L.R.James penned a flattering portrait of the ageing genius for the Manchester Guardian after witnessing his battles with Learie Constantine. The independent colonial spirit embodied by James was *"impressed by Barnes as a cricketer and a man"* he was later to pronounce in 'Beyond a Boundary', widely acclaimed as one of the best books about cricket ever written. *"What do they know of cricket that only cricket know?"*, asked James. Certainly Sydney Barnes had never let cricket interfere with the serious business of living.

As his appearances for Staffordshire decreased, so he

was to spend more time watching Test matches at Lord's, the citadel of cricket. Amongst his greatest admirers were Plum Warner and his wife. On seeing Barnes at the home of cricket, they would often introduce him to all the people who had so marvelled at the brilliance of his career and achievements. Barnes himself, however, although politely forthcoming in his sudden revisionism as icon rather than heretic, never let his newly-found fame go to his head. Ian Peebles testified that *"he is a man who does not welcome publicity and is certainly not one to boast"*. As one would expect of a leading ex-cricketer in the media explosion of the 1930's, Barnes acquired a position writing reports on Test cricket for a West Country newspaper. Even though he was now a member of the Fourth Estate, he was still acutely embarrassed by the flattery that was heaped upon him in the 1930's in the wake of the dominance of bat over ball. As Peebles was later to observe on writing about the greatness of Sydney Barnes: *"I have but one fear on publishing these remarks. As I have said, the subject is not a man who seeks or welcomes publicity, and I may well receive a severe reprimand."*

However, despite his apparent humility, the retired Sydney Barnes would have no qualms in making his views - on what he termed *"modern"* cricket - known. When England were playing Australia at Trent Bridge in 1948 he was heard to complain: *"Why do these bowlers send down so many balls the batsman needn't play? I didn't."* Later he was asked: *"Did you ever bowl full tosses?"* *"I never had the strength,"* was his disarming reply. His opinions spared neither bowler nor batsman: *"There is too much defensive bowling outside the leg stump and too much playing off the back foot,"* he was often heard to say. But his philosophy on cricket was refreshingly open and exciting and one which all lovers of the sport would have an affinity with: *"If you are going to get wickets, you must attack the batsman. If you are going to get runs, you must attack the bowler. That is the game of cricket."*

The aftermath of the Second World War could well have seen his reputation diminish. Instead, his fame spread further, right into the heart of an establishment which had been so quick to shun him nearly half a century earlier. In 1951 his accomplishments were finally recognised when he became one of the original honourary members of the M.C.C. In 1953 he became a life member of the Staffordshire Society in London, putting him in such distinguished company as Dr Samuel Johnson. In 1954 a portrait was commissioned from the famous Lancashire artist Harry Rutherford which still hangs at Lord's, the home of cricket, alongside such greats as W.G.Grace. Rutherford was in no doubt, despite his subject's eighty-one years, how Barnes spread terror amongst opposing batsmen. *"I don't know how the batsmen felt,"* he said, *"but he almost frightened me!"*

But, perhaps, his finest hours came during the celebrations surrounding his eightieth birthday in 1953. Jack Fingleton remembers the *"proud and erect figure"* who was guest of honour at a Cricket Writer's Dinner at Skinner's Hall in London a few days after his birthday, where the seventy-year-old Jack Hobbs was happy to share the stage with the great man. A testimonial match was held in his honour on the 26th April between two sides captained by Walter Robins and Geoff Edrich. The role call of England players appearing in the match was like a who's who of England Test cricket of the 1940's and 50's. Denis Compton, Norman Yardley, Bill Hollies, Jack Ikin, Charlie Palmer and Cyril Washbrook all appeared at this marvellous occasion on the ground of the Stafford club in front of a crowd of 5,000.

Barnes was to bowl the opening over. *"You had better give me an old ball,"* he chuckled, *"I might run through the other side with a new one and spoil your match!"* Amazingly, he felt so good after bowling that over - inevitably a maiden over - he promptly bowled another. John Hartley of The Times made this particularly telling observation of his physical condition at eighty, which gives a wonderful insight into why his cricket career lasted for so long: *"Barnes is neither frail nor infirm. Anyone seeing him striding easily and quickly each day up the long flight of steps to his office in the Shire Hall, Stafford, must be impressed by his vigour."*

Arthur Gilligan, an England captain during the inter-war years described him as *"a magnificent personality after his playing days."* Certainly, his opinions seem to have been much sought after. *"The LBW rule, as it is now, has done much harm to cricket,"* was an oft-repeated criticism by Barnes. *"If you are going to get wickets, you must attack the batsman,"* was another favourite mantra. On the post-war dominance of the Australians he was equally forthright: *"We should have beaten them years ago if we had attacked them."* And, of course the subject of Don Bradman was never far from his thoughts. Sydney Barnes would surely have relished the prospect of bowling at the greatest batsman of them all. *"He did not like one going away,"* was his assessment of The Don's weaknesses. It is possibly one of the great mistakes of all time that a confrontation between Barnes and Bradman was never arranged in the years after the appearance of the great Australian and whilst Barnes was still wheeling away for Staffordshire.

His eightieth year saw the renewal of the battle for the Ashes and Jack Fingleton reminisces on a meeting he had with Barnes late in the season at Stoke, when he was able to have *"a good old cricketers' yarn"*. That was, of course, until an official approached the master bowler and informed him that the Australian Prime Minister, Robert Menzies, was eager to meet him. *"I am still in the process of forgiving the Prime Minister!"* explained the disappointed Fingleton. In fact, Jack Fingleton sums up the feelings of his fellow cricket enthusiasts of the time by describing Barnes as *"courteous, gentle and gracious"*, with an *"alert and discerning"* mind. Barnes, modestly, even put his greatest achievement at

Melbourne in 1911 into a proper perspective to Fingleton: *"Naturally, I was very pleased, but I did not consider it the highlight of my career, for I knew it was possible to bowl well with little or no result. On the other hand, one could bowl not nearly so well and reap quite a harvest of wickets - you know as well as I do that there is a very small margin between success and failure."*

Bernard Hollowood provides a discordant note to this picture of amiability which Barnes had fostered for himself:

Cricketers and cricket writers who did not know him in his playing days have the strange idea that Barnes was always the genial, cryptic conversationalist of his octogenarian years, the familiar memorable figure who sat with the blind Wilfred Rhodes at Test matches, the dispenser of memorabilia and bonhomie. He wasn't. After a lifetime of groaning and bickering, Barnes began to enjoy the fame that had so long been denied him. His achievements were put into perspective and illuminated anew by the fantastic exploitation of cricket in the post-war years by radio, television, the press and book-publishing. He was feted, honoured, befriended, wined and dined, and he thoroughly enjoyed his belated helping of jam on his bread. It surprised him, this adulation, for hitherto he had assumed that he alone was aware of his genius. And I suppose he must often have wondered as the plaudits rolled forth how different his life would have been had he been able to 'fit in' and accept discipline in his playing days.

Although Hollowood is correct in implying that he would have achieved greater recognition had he accepted the master/servant relationship more readily, it is doubtful that it would have made him a better player. His conflict with the establishment merely spurred him on to perfection. Had he settled into the life of the full-time professional cricketer when he had his chance in the early years of the century, and undertook the routine which was followed by most of his peers, his effectiveness on the big occasion would almost certainly have been diminished. His record at the very highest level is far superior to any of his contemporaries and, on the evidence of his two seasons of county cricket, there were players performing at the time who were as - or even more - prolific. But they did not go on to supreme feats like those of Barnes in Australia in 1911/12 and South Africa in 1913/14.

Neville Cardus, to celebrate the centenary of Wisden in 1963, selected *"Six Giants of the Wisden Century".* Inevitably, Sydney Barnes was one of those six. It must surely have filled the old man with a glowing pride to see himself ranked alongside the likes of W.G.Grace, Don Bradman, Jack Hobbs, Victor Trumper and Tom Richardson. He was now plainly one of cricket's immortals and Cardus, the foremost commentator on the game of the 20th Century, had no doubts: *"Most cricketers and students of the game belonging to the period in which S.F. Barnes played were agreed that he was the bowler of the century."* A multitude of cricket enthusiasts from all over the world were to search him out right up until his death in 1967. Initially reticent in the company of yet another admirer who had never seen his greatest exhibitions, he would eventually settle down and reminisce with fascinating stories of his wonderful deeds. Perhaps the ultimate accolade was paid to him in 1965 when the Sydney Barnes Cricket Society was formed. There is no better memorial to his incredible career than a group formed solely to appraise his achievements.

In 1957 he had become the first honourary life member of Staffordshire County Cricket Club, whilst in 1961 he attended a dinner of surviving Test cricketers from Ashes series, in which he was the eldest at 89. At the age of ninety he was elected as President of the Warwickshire Old County Cricketers Association. At the age of ninety-two he had a bad fall, breaking some ribs, and the cricket world held its breath. His many thousands of admirers around the world cheered heartily as he made a full recovery in Staffordshire Royal Infirmary. He died at home on the Boxing Day of 1967, admired as a man far removed from the lonely and despised figure that many critics had predicted for him in the early years of the century. He was cremated and his ashes are housed in the pavilion at Edgbaston, where he had made his first class debut seventy-three years earlier.

For lovers of the game the abiding image was of the popular and recognisable figure at Lord's Test matches in the 1950's and 60's. Accompanied by the now blind Wilfred Rhodes - his antithesis in character, but equal in achievement and longevity - this pair of talismans of the Golden Age inspired the poet-cricketer Alan Ross to this timeless and evocative piece of verse:

> *Then, elbows linked but straight as sailors*
> *on a tilting deck, they move.*
> *One square-shouldered as a tailor's*
> *Model, leans over, whispering in the other's ear.*
> *Go easy. Steps here. This end bowling.'*
> *Turning, I watch Barnes guide Rhodes into fresher air,*
> *as if to continue an innings, though Rhodes may only*
> *play by ear.*

17.

THE GREATEST BOWLER OF ALL TIME

The death of Sydney Barnes in 1967 prompted the M.C.C. Secretary, S.C.Griffith, to make this comment: *"The extraordinary thing about him was that all his contemporaries considered him the greatest bowler. There was never any doubts in their minds. This must have been unique."* Apart from the irony of such praise coming from an official of an organisation that did so much to stifle his early career, it is certainly a statement based in fact. One statistic alone, his 189 wickets in 27 Tests at an average of 16.43, a figure far in excess of any of his predecessors or contemporaries, proves this beyond doubt.

Before the advent of Barnes on the international cricket scene there had been several prolific performers. For Australia, the Demon Spofforth took ninety-four wickets in Ashes tests, whilst C.T.B.Turner managed 101 and George Giffen 103. Both took their wickets at a comparable rate to Sydney Barnes. However, the careers of Spofforth, Turner and Giffen encompassed the period between 1876 and 1895, immediately before the Golden Age. One reason why the period between 1895 and 1914 is called the *"Golden Age"* is that batsmanship improved because the state of the wickets which were played on bore no relation to those of the first twenty years of Test cricket. Groundsmen adopted modern techniques for cultivating grass that were more conducive to even bounce, whilst the heavy roller only came into widespread usage in the 1890's. As a result, the achievements of Spofforth, Turner and Giffen, as well as those of Johnnie Briggs, Bobbie Peel and George Lohmann, the three England bowlers who had taken over 100 Test wickets before Barnes came on the scene, and Tom Richardson, who took eighty-eight wickets, can be put into a proper perspective as inferior to that of Sydney Barnes. Lohmann is the only Test bowler to have a lower average than Barnes. In fact, his 112 wickets cost an amazing 10.75 apiece. A large proportion of those wickets, however, were taken against the extremely weak South African teams of the 1880's and 1890's.

What of Barnes' contemporaries? The outstanding Australian bowlers were Hugh Trumble and Monty Noble, with 141 and 121 Test wickets respectively. For England, Wilfred Rhodes' 121 Test wickets and Colin Blythe's 100 provided Barnes with the most reliable support. Trumble, Noble, Rhodes and Blythe were undoubtedly great bowlers who graced the Golden Age and troubled even the best of batsmen from time to time, but the cost of their wickets was significantly in excess of that of Sydney Barnes. Only Blythe of this quartet took their wickets at less than twenty apiece.

It is noticeable, in the comparison with the great bowlers of the first forty years of Test cricket, that Barnes' aggregate of wickets is notably greater than any other. This is a truly astonishing statistic considering the number of times he was either disregarded or injured during his Test career. In fact, excluding the chance he had to increase his total after the First World War, from his debut in 1901 until 1914 he missed no less than thirty-one of the fifty-eight Tests that England played in that period. One can only wonder what sort of record he would have created had he appeared for England in those other games. It is possible that he would have created a record which may never have been beaten, despite the amount of Test cricket that is played in the modern era. Little wonder that in the Wisden eulogy of 1910 it is stated: *"The Australian batsmen were never in any doubt as to his class"*, and, in describing his part in the 1907/8 tour, it says: *"As on the occasion of his previous visit he won golden opinions in Australia, M.A.Noble describing him as the best bowler in the world."*

What of the great bowlers of the inter-war years? For England, Maurice Tate, Hedley Verity and Harold Larwood played many more Tests than Barnes and failed to capture anywhere near as many wickets. Of course, they played on the superb wickets of the late 1920's and 1930's and bowled against Bradman and Ponsford in their prime but, even so, their records bear no comparison to that of Sydney Barnes.

The two great and prolific Australian bowlers of that era are a different proposition. Clarrie Grimmett, who announced himself in international cricket with eleven for 82 in the final Test of England's 1924/5 tour of Australia, was the first man to overhaul Barnes' total of 189 Test wickets. In an almost mirror image of Sydney Barnes' performance twenty-three years earlier he took forty-four wickets on his final tour in South Africa in 1935/6, including ten wickets in a match in three consecutive Tests. His final total, however, of 216 Test wickets took ten Tests more than Barnes at an average of nearly ten runs a wicket more. It is said of Grimmett that he had to bowl at Hobbs, Hammond and Sutcliffe in their prime. But Barnes had to deal with Trumper, Hill, Darling, Macartney, Armstrong, Noble, Kelleway and Bardsley in theirs. In fact, the strength and depth of Australia's batting in the Golden Age was undoubtedly greater than England's in Grimmett's time, and, in any case, Grimmett was far more successful in England and South Africa than in his native Australia, where Barnes excelled.

Much the same can be said of Bill O'Reilly, but the comparison with Sydney Barnes is more potent because no less an authority than Don Bradman reckoned that O'Reilly

184

must have been a better bowler than Barnes. The statistics, however, do not back up Bradman's argument. Although O'Reilly played the same number of Tests as Barnes, twenty-seven, and was just as successful in Australia as elsewhere, he took forty-five fewer wickets at an average in excess of twenty-two. Moreover, an analysis of the victims of O'Reilly, and Grimmett for that matter, show that the majority of their wickets were batsmen in the lower part of the order. They were change bowlers who often came on after the openers had taken out England or South Africa's best batsman.

For Sydney Barnes, as an opening bowler, there was no hiding place from the best that Australia and South Africa could offer and a look at his victims in Test cricket prove this beyond doubt. No bowler ever accounted for Victor Trumper as many times as Barnes. On thirteen occasions, usually for a single figure score, this majestic batsman became Barnes' victim. Clem Hill was dismissed eleven times, Vernon Ransford and Herbie Taylor, who supposedly tamed the master bowler in South Africa in 1913/14, were taken eight times. Warren Bardsley, Herbie Carter, Syd Gregory, Warwick Armstrong and David Nourse fell six times. Charlie Macartney, Monty Noble and Aubrey Faulkner five times. These great batsmen alone represent almost half of Sydney Barnes' total of Test victims.

It is appropriate now to quote the views of players who straddled the Golden Age and the inter-war years, and who would have had first-hand knowledge of Barnes, Grimmett and O'Reilly. The greatest of these must surely have been Jack Hobbs. He made his Test debut in the same match that Barnes returned from his four-year exile, in Australia in 1907, and played his final game for England at the Oval in 1930. He is still the highest aggregate run scorer for England in Ashes Tests with 3,636 at an average of nearly fifty-five. He had this to say:

Syd Barnes, S.F., I've always put right at the top. He was the best bowler ever. I don't think even now there was anybody better, although I admit there were others almost his equal, like Bill O'Reilly. Syd hated batsmen. He had the leg-break, the off-break, and he was fast, tall and made the ball get up to unpleasant heights. He was lethal on matting in South Africa, and in Australia, 1911/ 12, he was marvellous.

Barnes, in return, paid Hobbs the handsome compliment of describing him as the best batsman in the world. Leslie Duckworth witnessed a magnificent century from Hobbs against Barnes in a Bradford League game during the First World War and described Barnes's face getting *"blacker and blacker and I was torn between suffering with him and exulting in such batting as I had never seen before in my young life."* Asked once which batsman gave him the most difficulty he explained that to Jack Hobbs one had to *"just plug them down"* at him and *"hope he would have a fit or something"*.

Cec Parkin, England's best bowler after the First World War, described Barnes as *"the greatest bowler of all times"* and that it was *"impossible for him to bowl bad balls"*, whilst Herbert Strudwick, the best wicket-keeper of the era, said of him: *"He was the greatest bowler I ever kept wicket to, for he sent down something different each ball of the over."* Arthur Gilligan, captain of the England touring team to Australia in 1924/5, was in no doubt as to the hegemony of Sydney Barnes. Writing in Barnes' obituary in the Wisden of 1968 he says, quite simply, *"He was the finest bowler there ever was."*

An oft-repeated accusation against Barnes was that he was inconsistent and performed only at certain venues. However, the facts do not bear this out at all. At Melbourne, supposedly a ground at which he tried his hardest and had his greatest successes, as well as being generally regarded as the best batting wicket in the world, he took thirty-five wickets in five Tests, an average of seven per game, exactly the same as his overall average. At Sydney and Adelaide he was only marginally less successful with twenty-eight wickets in five Tests and fourteen in three respectively. At Leeds he took seventeen in two Tests, at the Oval twenty-two in three Tests, at Lord's eleven in two Tests, at Sheffield seven in one and six in one at Manchester, although he played in one other Test there without bowling. And then, of course, there were his record-breaking performances in South Africa. His 83 Test wickets against South Africa has still not been surpassed. The fact of the matter was that he only seemed inconsistent because of the erratic behaviour of the selectors. Certainly no Australian batsman of the Golden Age has ever declared Barnes to have been easier to play on one day than another, as evidenced by Charlie Macartney's description of him as *"top class on all wickets."*

What of the great bowlers of the post-Second World War era? The proliferation of Test cricket after the Second World War has seen Sydney Barnes' aggregate of Test wickets submerged in a sea of statistics. It is incredible to find, however, that Barnes still ranks in eighth place in the all-time Test wicket-takers for England, and only Bob Willis, Ian Botham and Wilfred Rhodes have taken more wickets for England against Australia. Moreover, Barnes' seventy-seven wickets in Australia is still the highest by any non-Australian bowler. Immediately above him in the aggregate wicket-takers for England is the name of Jim Laker, with 193. Laker, of course, deprived Barnes of his record of seventeen wickets in a Test with his stunning nineteen for 90 at Old Trafford in 1956. But Laker's grand total took nearly twenty Tests more to overhaul that of Barnes; and nobody could argue that Barnes ever had conditions and luck in his favour in the way that Laker had at that Old Trafford Test.

In fact, whereas Barnes averaged seven wickets a game, no other bowler since the war has averaged more than five.

Nor can anyone argue that Barnes was the only bowler England had at the time and had more opportunity to take wickets. With the likes of Wilfred Rhodes, Colin Blythe, Bill Lockwood, Stanley Jackson, George Hirst, Frank Foster, Frank Woolley and Arthur Fielder around, there was no shortage of competition for victims. All teams since the first official Test in 1877 have had a variety of bowlers; Sydney Barnes merely had a greater number of ways of taking wickets.

Even though over thirty international bowlers have now taken more wickets than Sydney Barnes, there is one statistic where he still remains, remarkably, in the top three in the all-time list. In his twenty-seven Tests Sydney Barnes took five wickets in an innings on no less than twenty-three occasions. Of the thirty bowlers who have taken more than 200 Test wickets only two, Richard Hadlee with thirty-six and Ian Botham with twenty-seven, have achieved this particular feat more times. Furthermore, only Hadlee, with nine, has taken ten wickets in a match more times than Sydney Barnes' seven. When one considers that Hadlee has taken 431 wickets in 86 Tests, and Botham 383 in 102 Tests, it merely shows what an amazing bowler Barnes was. When C.L.R.James called him *"the greatest of all bowlers"*, he was making no idle claim, whilst Denzil Batchelor, in his 'The Book of Cricket', does not exaggerate when he describes Barnes as *"the bowler against whom Australians and South Africans will measure your latter day genius - and find that the newcomer falls short."*

Let us not forget his performances in minor cricket because, even though it was a lower standard than first class cricket, it is hard to believe than any other bowler in the history of the game could have performed any better. 1,441 wickets at 8.15 for Staffordshire in twenty-three seasons over thirty-one years strains credulity to its limits, especially considering all those wickets were taken after his thirtieth birthday and almost 40% after the age of fifty. This is a record which will never be broken. Then, in league cricket, against teams with other international cricketers and league players who saw it as their duty to try their hardest when facing the opposition's professional, his total of 4,069 wickets at 6.08 is nothing short of astounding. His county cricket average of under twenty with 226 wickets was eminently respectable considering he retired from this form of cricket when just getting into his stride, whilst his 304 wickets at 15.13 in other representative games, at a level only marginally below Test standard, compares favourably with any other bowler in any era.

There is constant debate over who was the greatest batsman of all time. Bradman on the basis of statistics, Hobbs for consistency, Hammond and Sobers for style, Trumper for inventiveness, Richards and Macartney for destructiveness. And then there is Brian Lara of modern players, who has recently broken Test and first class individual scoring records. It is a debate that has raged for decades. But for bowlers there can be no such contention. Who else has been picked for their national team to such devastating effect after a handful of moderately successful first class games over a period of seven years? Who else was still playing as a professional at the age of sixty-seven? Who else has commanded a successful professional cricket career over forty-five years? Who else has advertised themselves as available for a professional contract at the age of fifty-five and received a large number of replies? On all measurable indices Sydney Francis Barnes is the greatest bowler there has ever been. The last word goes to the distinguished historian H.S. Altham, who was unequivocal in his vote for Barnes as the greatest bowler of all time:

Art, resolution, stamina, he commanded them all. Well might a man who saw him in his prime have found himself saying: 'Here was Caesar! When comes such another?'

Appendices

Appendix A

S.F.BARNES - CAREER RECORDS

	Overs	Maidens	Runs	Wickets	Average
Test Matches	1,312.2	358	3,106	189	16.43
Other First Class	4,078.4	1,205	9,034	530	17.05
Staffordshire	5,457.3	1,647	11,754	1,441	8.15
League	12,802	3,532	27,974	4,069	6.08
TOTALS	**23,509.3**	**6,784**	**51,890**	**6,229**	**8.33**

Appendix B

S.F.BARNES - TEST MATCH PERFORMANCES

	Opposition/Venue/Date/Result	Analysis
1	V.AUSTRALIA Sydney-Dec13/14/16 1901 (won by inns & 124 runs)	35.1-9-65-5 16-2-74-1
2	V.AUSTRALIA Melbourne-Dec1/2/3/4 1902 (lost by 229 runs)	16.1-5-42-6 64-17-121-7
3	V.AUSTRALIA Adelaide-Jan17/18/20/21/22/23 1902 (lost by 4 wkts)	7-0-21-0
5	V.AUSTRALIA Sydney-Dec13/14/16/17/18/19 1907 (lost by 2 wkts)	22-3-74-1 30-7-63-2
6	V.AUSTRALIA Melbourne-Jan1/2/3/4/6/7 1908 (won by 1 wkt)	17-7-30-0 27.4-4-72-5
7	V.AUSTRALIA Adelaide-Jan10/11/13/14/15/16 1908 (lost by 245 runs)	27-8-60-3 42-9-83-3
8	V.AUSTRALIA Melbourne-Feb7/8/10/11 1908 (lost by 308 runs)	23-11-37-1 35-13-69-1
9	V.AUSTRALIA Sydney-Feb21/22/24/25/26/27 1908 (lost by 49 runs)	22.4-6-60-7 27-6-78-1
10	V.AUSTRALIA Leeds-July1/2/3 1909 (lost by 126 runs)	25-12-37-1 35-18-63-6
11	V.AUSTRALIA Manchester-July26/27/28 1909 (match drawn)	27-9-56-5 22.3-5-66-1
12	V.AUSTRALIA Oval-Aug9/10/11 1909 (match drawn)	19-3-57-2 27-7-61-2
13	V.AUSTRALIA Sydney-Dec15/16/18/19/20/21 1911 (lost by 146 runs)	35-5-107-3 30-8-72-1

	Opposition/Venue/Date/Result	Analysis
14	V.AUSTRALIA Melbourne-Dec30/Jan1/2/3 1911/12 (won by 8 wkts)	23-9-44-5 32.1-7-96-3
15	V.AUSTRALIA Adelaide-Jan12/13/15/16/17 1912 (won by 7 wkts)	23-4-71-3 46.4-7-105-5
16	V.AUSTRALIA Melbourne-Feb9/10/12/13 1912 (won by inns and 225 runs)	29.1-4-74-5 20-6-47-2
17	V.AUSTRALIA Sydney-Feb23/24/26/27/28/29 1912 (won by 70 runs)	19-2-56-3 39-12-106-4
18	V.SOUTH AFRICA Lord's-Jun10/11/12 1912 (won by inns and 62 runs)	13-3-25-5 34-9-85-6
19	V.AUSTRALIA Lord's-Jun24/25/26 1912 (match drawn)	31-10-74-0
20	V.SOUTH AFRICA Leeds-July8/9/10 1912 (won by 174 runs)	22-7-52-6 21.2-5-63-4
21	V.AUSTRALIA Manchester-July 29/30/31 1912 (match drawn)	
22	V.SOUTH AFRICA Oval-Aug12/13 1912 (won by 10 wkts)	21-10-28-5 16.4-4-29-8
23	V.AUSTRALIA Oval-Aug19/20/21/22 1912 (won by 244 runs)	27-15-30-5 4-1-18-0
24	V.SOUTH AFRICA Durban-Dec13/15/16/17 1913 (won by inns and 157 runs)	19.4-1-57.5 25-11-48-5
25	V.SOUTH AFRICA Johannesburg-Dec26/27/29/30 1913 (won by inns and 12 runs)	26.5-9-56-8 38.4-7-103-9
26	V.SOUTH AFRICA Johannesburg-Jan1/2/3/5 1914 (won by 91 runs)	16-3-26-3 34-8-102-5
27	V.SOUTH AFRICA Durban-Jan14/16/17/18 1914 (match drawn)	29.5-7-56-7 32-10-88-7

APPENDIX C

S.F.BARNES - TEST MATCH VICTIMS

NAME	Bowled	Caught	LBW	Stumped	Hit Wkt	TOTAL
V.T.Trumper(A)	5	8				13
C.Hill(A)	4	7				11
V.S.Ransford(A)	2	4	2			8
H.W.Taylor(SA)	2	2	4			8
W.W.Armstrong(A)	3	2	1			6
W.Bardsley(A)	3	2	1			6
H.Carter(A)	1	3	2			6
S.E.Gregory(A)	1	5				6
A.D.Nourse(SA)	3	2			1	6
G.A.Faulkner(SA)	3	2				5
G.P.D.Hartigan(SA)	1	3	1			5
C.G.Macartney(A)	3	2				5
M.A.Noble(A)	2	3				5
L.J.Tancred(SA)	2	1		2		5
R.Beaumont(SA)	2	2				4
A.Cotter(A)	3	1				4
J.Darling(A)		4				4
J.L.Cox(SA)	2	2				4
P.A.M.Hands(SA)		4				4
T.J.Matthews(A)	1	3				4
R.B.Minnett(A)		4				4
C.J.Newberry(SA)	1	1		2		4
T.A.Ward(SA)	3	1				4
E.Jones(A)		3				3
C.B.Llewellyn(SA)	1	2				3
S.J.Snooke(SA)	2	1				3
C.P.Carter(SA)	1	1				2

194

NAME	Bowled	Caught	LBW	Stumped	Hit Wkt	TOTAL
A.H.C.Cooper(SA)	1	1				2
R.A.Duff(A)		2				2
H.V.Hordern(A)	1	1				2
W.P.Howell(A)	1	1				2
C.Kelleway(A)	1		1			2
J.J.Kelly(A)	1	1				2
F.Le Roux(SA)	1	1				2
P.T.Lewis(SA)		2				2
P.A.McAlister(A)		2				2
F.Mitchell(SA)	1	1				2
J.A.O'Connor(A)	1	1				2
S.J.Pegler(SA)	2					2
R.O.Schwarz(SA)	1	1				2
L.A.Stricker(SA)	1	1				2
D.Taylor(SA)		2				2
H.Trumble(A)		2				2
G.C.White(SA)	1	1				2
J.W.Zulch(SA)		2				2
J.W.Blanckenberg(SA)		1				1
T.Campbell(SA)		1				1
H.W.Chapman(SA)	1					1
C.D.Dixon(SA)		1				1
R.J.Hartigan(A)		1				1
G.R.Hazlitt(A)	1					1
A.J.Hopkins(A)		1				1
C.E.McLeod(A)	1					1
J.V.Saunders(A)		1				1
L.G.Tapscott(SA)	1					1
L.R.Tuckett(SA)	1					1
W.J.Whitty(A)		1				1
TOTALS	69	103	12	4	1	189
PERCENTAGES	36.5	54.5	6.5	2	0.5	100

APPENDIX D
S.F.BARNES - ALL FIRST CLASS

Year	Overs	Maidens	Runs	Wickets	Average
1895	55	15	145	3	48.3
1896	23	8	54	-	-
1899	75	28	161	4	40.25
1901	36	8	99	6	16.5
1901/2(Aus)	285.4	51	676	41	16.48
1902	834.5	242	2,049	95	21.56
1903	1,023	363	2,339	131	17.85
1907/8(Aus)	534	145	1,185	54	21.94
1909	250.3	83	537	34	15.79
1911	132.5	39	350	14	25
1911/12(Aus)	659.2	108	1,231	59	20.86
1912	386.4	137	782	69	11.33
1913	147.1	50	351	35	10.02
1913/14(SA)	449.2	128	1,118	104	10.75
1914	48	13	144	8	18
1924	16	3	32	5	6.4
1927	43	12	77	4	19.25
1928	97	29	205	20	10.25
1929	237.4	83	465	29	16.03
1930	57	18	140	4	35
TOTALS	**5,391**	**1,563**	**12,140**	**719**	**16.88**

APPENDIX E
S.F.BARNES - STAFFORDSHIRE CAREER RECORD

YEAR	Overs	Maidens	Runs	Wickets	Average
1904	269.4	62	679	66	10.28
1905	193.2	44	508	44	11.54
1906	373.1	100	932	119	7.83
1907	246	82	505	79	6.39
1908	397.4	139	817	92	8.88
1909	285	85	676	93	7.26
1910	363.5	99	879	90	9.76
1911	337.2	113	750	104	7.21
1912	191	75	376	70	5.37
1913	196.3	48	397	65	6.1
1914	159.3	57	297	48	6.18
1924	256.5	79	525	73	7.19
1925	184.5	57	417	31	13.45
1926	312.2	98	624	76	8.21
1927	253.2	81	493	81	6.08
1928	215.4	70	404	55	7.34
1929	291.4	83	565	68	8.3
1930	165.1	56	293	51	5.74
1931	241.5	77	523	61	8.57
1932	268.3	76	505	56	9.01
1933	108	31	222	7	31.71
1934	56	17	113	3	37.66
1935	90.2	18	255	9	28.33
TOTALS	5,457.3	1,647	11,755	1,441	8.15

APPENDIX F
S.F.BARNES - LEAGUE CRICKET CAREER

Year	Club	League	Ovs	Mdns	Runs	Wkts	Ave
1895	Rishton	Lancashire	347	97	705	71	9.92
1896	Rishton	Lancashire	406	95	959	85	11.28
1897	Rishton	Lancashire	382	115	753	87	8.65
1898	Rishton	Lancashire	373	113	813	96	8.46
1899	Rishton	Lancashire	314	81	760	72	10.55
1900	Burnley	Lancashire	436.2	120	1,024	111	9.22
1901	Burnley	Lancashire	362	86	925	114	8.11
1904	Church	Lancashire	260.3	57	636	64	9.93
1905	Church	Lancashire	330.3	79	815	90	9.05
1906	Porthill Park	North Staffs	256.3	79	530	103	5.14
1907	Porthill Park	North Staffs	216.5	63	439	112	3.91
1908	Porthill Park	North Staffs	352.1	133	693	122	5.68
1909	Porthill Park	North Staffs	224.5	76	428	100	4.28
1910	Porthill Park	North Staffs	252.3	93	476	82	5.8
1911	Porthill Park	North Staffs	306	77	792	109	7.62
1912	Porthill Park	North Staffs	213	70	395	66	6.98
1913	Porthill Park	North Staffs	240.5	73	532	114	4.66
1914	Porthill Park	North Staffs	209	71	434	85	5.1

Year	Club	League	Ovs	Mdns	Runs	Wkts	Ave
1915	Saltaire	Bradford	108	40	407	92	4.42
1916	Saltaire	Bradford	251	53	603	93	6.48
1917	Saltaire	Bradford	233.3	57	527	107	4.92
1918	Saltaire	Bradford	236	60	583	112	5.2
1919	Saltaire	Bradford	212	62	576	68	8.47
1920	Saltaire	Bradford	265	90	536	100	5.36
1921	Saltaire	Bradford	292.4	71	638	112	5.69
1922	Saltaire	Bradford	311	80	618	150	4.11
1923	Saltaire	Bradford	150.1	49	269	70	3.84
1924	Castleton Moor	Central Lancs	268.2	67	581	90	6.45
1925	Castleton Moor	Central Lancs	432.1	132	820	136	6.02
1926	Castleton Moor	Central Lancs	348.3	108	677	113	5.99
1927	Castleton Moor	Central Lancs	303	92	608	119	5.1
1928	Castleton Moor	Central Lancs	344	97	804	125	6.43
1929	Rochdale	Central Lancs	367.5	100	755	114	6.62
1930	Rochdale	Central Lancs	331.4	80	732	89	8.22
1931	Rawtenstall	Lancashire	333.4	94	725	115	6.3
1932	Rawtenstall	Lancashire	440.3	159	819	113	7.25
1933	Rawtenstall	Lancashire	275.2	62	741	54	13.72
1934	Keighley	Bradford	413.4	122	891	86	10.36
1935	Smethwick	Birmingham	298	86	649	75	8.65
1936	Smethwick	Birmingham	174	37	438	38	11.52
1937	Lytham St Annes	Ribblesdale	516.2	69	761	61	12.47
1938	Bridgnorth	non-league	336	77	875	126	6.94
1940	Stone	N. Staffs & S.Chesh.	76.4	10	232	28	8.28
		TOTALS	12,802	3,532	27,974	4,069	6.08

BIBLIOGRAPHY

WISDEN CRICKETERS' ALMANACK 1895-97, 1900, 1902-35, 1963, 1968, 1994 (John Wisden & Co. Ltd.)

S.F.BARNES, Master Bowler - Leslie Duckworth (The Sportsmans Book Club 1968)

SYDNEY BARNES, The Greatest Bowler of All Time - Wilfrid S. White (E.F.Hudson 1935)

A HISTORY OF COUNTY CRICKET - Lancashire - John Kay (Arthur Barker Ltd. 1972)

FROM THE STRETFORD END, The Official History of Lancashire C.C.C. - Brian Bearshaw (Partridge Press 1990)

LANCASHIRE COUNTY CRICKET 1864-1953 - A.W.Ledbrooke (Phoenix House Ltd. 1954)

RED ROSES CREST THE CAPS, The Story of Lancashire County Cricket Club - Eric Midwinter (Kingswood Press 1989)

THE HISTORY OF LANCASHIRE COUNTY CRICKET CLUB - Peter Wynne-Thomas (Christopher Helm 1989)

OLD TRAFFORD - John Marshall (Pelham Books 1971)

ARCHIE - Michael Down (George Allen & Unwin 1981)

FIFTY YEARS REMINISCENCES OF A NON-PLAYER - W.E.Howard (Old Trafford 1928)

A HISTORY OF THE COUNTY CRICKET CHAMPIONSHIP - Robert Brooke (Guinness Publishing 1991)

A HISTORY OF CRICKET - Benny Green (Barrie & Jenkins 1988)

THE GOLDEN AGE OF CRICKET - George Plumtre (Queen Anne Press 1990)

A HISTORY OF AUSTRALIAN CRICKET - Chris Harte (Andre Deutsch 1993)

A HISTORY OF CRICKET - Trevor Bailey (George Allen & Unwin 1978)

HISTORY OF THE TESTS - Sydney Smith (The Australian Publishing Co. 1946)

SINS OF OMISSION, The Story of The Test Selectors 1899-1990 - Allen Synge (Pelham Books 1990)

THE PLAYERS, A Social History of the Professional Cricketer - Ric Sissons (The Kingswood Press 1988)

200

THE BOWLER'S ART, Understanding Spin, Swing and Swerve - Brian Wilkins (A & C Black 1991)

LORD'S 1787-1945 - Sir Pelham Warner (George G. Harrap 1946)

MASTERS OF CRICKET, From Trumper to May - Jack Fingleton (Pavilion Books 1990)

DOUBLE CENTURY, Cricket in The Times, Volume Two 1935-1990 - Edited by Marcus Williams (Pavilion Books 1990)

TALKING OF CRICKET - Ian Peebles (Museum Press 1953)

THE ENGLISH GAME - compiled by Gerald Brodribb (Hollis and Carter 1948)

CRICKET ON THE BRAIN - Bernard Hollowood (Eyre & Spottiswoode 1970)

CRICKETERS CARNIVAL - Learie Constantine (Stanley Paul)

BEYOND A BOUNDARY - C.L.R.James (Stanley Paul 1990)

SEE THE CONQUERING HERO, The Story of the Lancashire League 1892-1992 - Dave Edmundson (Mike McLeod 1992)

THE GREATEST SHOW ON TURF, Centenary of the Lancashire League - Noel Wild (Hendon Publishing 1992)

PLAY RESUMED WITH CARDUS - Neville Cardus (Souvenir Press 1979)

FOR THE LOVE OF THE GAME, An Oral History of Cricket - David Lemmon (Michael Joseph 1993)

PAVILIONED IN SPLENDOUR - A.A.Thomson (Pavilion Books 1990)

SPORT AND THE BRITISH, A Modern History - Richard Hill (Oxford University Press 1989)

ANYONE BUT ENGLAND, Cricket and the National Malaise - Michael Marqusee (Verso 1994)

Newspapers and Periodicals:

The Sporting Chronicle
Manchester Evening News
Daily Mirror
Daily Express
The Cricketer
The Times

INDEX

202

204